WRITERS' WORKSHOP SERIES

How to teach fiction writing at key stage 2

PIE CORBETT

David Fulton Publishers

London

David Fulton Publishers Ltd
The Chiswick Centre, 414 Chiswick High Road, London W4 5TF

www.fultonpublishers.co.uk

First published in Great Britain by David Fulton Publishers 2001
Reprinted 2002 (twice)

British Library Publication Data
A catalogue record for this book is available from the British Library

ISBN 1-85346-833-9

Also available in the **Writers' Workshop Series:**

How to teach writing across the curriculum at key stage 2   ISBN 1-85346-803-7
How to teach poetry writing at key stage 2   ISBN 1-85346-804-5

Dedicated to all those in teaching who fly the
flag of creativity and imagination, without
which we are nothing.

Edited by Dodi Beardshaw
Page design by Ken Vail Graphic Design
Cover photographs by John Redman
Typeset by FiSH Books, London
Printed in Great Britain by Bell and Bain Ltd, Glasgow

Contents

Introduction

Why stories matter

Reading stories is magic. Everyone knows that. Reading a good story takes us into another world where anything can happen. Lost in that other place we see the words on the page, yet in our minds we live the story in a stronger place – the imagination.

Writing stories is also magic. Lost in the act of writing we can create that other place and watch our characters acting out their story. Nico, aged 7, said, 'What I like about writing is that you never quite know what is going to happen.' It is this sense of the story as a journey of discovery – finding a tale to be told, and being lead forward to its conclusion – that seems so satisfying.

Story helps us understand our lives – to explain who we are, what has happened to us and what might happen. Much of the time we make a story out of what has happened to us, or we imagine forwards the story of what might happen. Narrative is like a template that we place upon our lives, so that we can understand our selves, and our world. It is through narrative that we can step out of the darkness of ourselves. As such, it is more important than any crude levelling process. It is to do with the genuine functions of education.

How to use this book

This book is intended to be a handbook for teachers at KS2. It provides ideas for writing workshops, covering the main aspects of story writing. Whilst each section does reflect objectives in the national literacy framework, the book can be used flexibly by any teacher to develop different aspects of narrative writing. There are suggested activities and texts to use for demonstration writing or for class discussion. All this should be richly supplemented by the current stories that the class are reading.

The book is written so that the teacher can teach straight from the manual, using the examples given. These can be made slightly easier or a little more demanding, depending on the class. Some workshops may provide enough content for a number of sessions, others may prove to be sufficient for one session. The basic ideas are such that they can be repeated in different year groups.

The writing journal

'It didn't occur to me that you wrote about what you knew, and that the material of poets was simply under your nose.' (Charles Causley) It still remains true that we write best about what we know. What else can we write about? Every writer that I have met uses a notebook or journal for jotting down ideas – things overheard, strange sights, snippets of conversation, mannerisms, intriguing thoughts, observations of daily life. Some of this finds its way back into their writing, so that they use their observation of the real and weave this into imagining what might happen if...? Anne Fine says 'Often I think, "what if...?" What if people came to our planet and wanted to eat us roasted, and fried and baked?' Theresa Breslin comments that 'all my books start with real incidents'.

It may be helpful, therefore, for children to keep a writing journal to store useful ideas, suggestions, writing tips, word lists – anything that might be useful to support their writing – lists of powerful verbs, speech verbs, how to set out dialogue, used tips about characterisation, lists of connectives, words I keep misspelling, basic plot ideas and so on. The journal should be to hand whenever the children write – and they should refer to it in order to assist their writing. The journal can also act like an artist's sketchbook – it is both a store of possibilities as well as a testing ground. Ideas for stories might be collected, and unusual characters or places, interesting events and memories.

Collecting good scraps

Betsy Byars says in her autobiography *The Moon and Me* that 'plenty of good scraps are as important in making a book as in the making of a quilt. I often think of my books as scrapbooks of my life, because I put in them all the neat things that I see and read and hear. I sometimes wonder what people who don't write do with all their good stuff.' Her scraps are the many things that we notice, that intrigue for a moment and, unless you are a writer, may be rapidly forgotten. They do not have to be dramatic events – very often it is detail, a turn of phrase, the way a man holds his mobile phone. Ted Hughes wrote that, 'you write interestingly only about things that genuinely interest you.' Well, here are some of the scraps that have recently interested me:

- Overheard in Waterstone's: a strident voice saying, 'I'm looking for Ernest Hemingway.' Being tempted to answer, 'Sorry Miss, he's just nipped out.'
- A black cat running through an estate with a goldfish in its mouth.
- An old woman with plastic rugby balls in her bags.
- A sausage dog in a carrier bag that sang in church.
- A tortoise found on a motorway.

Writers are magpies

One of the best ways to crush creativity is to believe that children do not have experiences worth writing about. This viewpoint suggests that the children's lives are worthless; if we devalue their world we devalue who they are. Their experiences may not be what we would wish for – but all children's lives are a red-hot resource of experience, a seedbed for their writing. We have to help children become magpies and steal from their own lives – to use places they know, people they know, events that they know, feelings that they know. As Charles Bukowski said, 'I have nothing to invent.' I think, though, that writers are different from the rest of us in three ways:

1. they notice when something happens that might be useful within their own writing;
2. they value their own experiences and see them as potential source for writing;
3. they write these 'scraps' of experience down – or remember them – ready to use them as a resource.

In this way the 'writing journal' becomes a great storehouse of ideas and language. Without this, many writers would be impoverished, clutching at straws in the wind. Children also need to keep some sort of writing journal. Anne Fine agrees; 'You learn to recognise what sort of thing can make a story or fit in a book. You find yourself thinking, "I can use that".'

Running a writing workshop

This book is built around a basic model of teaching writing, centred upon the idea that we develop as writers through reading with a writer's eye. Whenever we sit down to write, all experiences will help to inform the writing, providing a great storehouse of characters, places and events. Calling on this storehouse can help young writers. Looking at good quality examples of writing and working out how the writer managed to gain an impact is also a useful writing strategy. Look at how the best writers set about the task and then attempt to write in the same vein. The sequence for teaching used in this book is flexible:

1. Look at some examples.
2. Analyse how they were written.
3. Discuss how the writer achieved the impact.
4. The teacher demonstrates as a writer.
5. The teacher acts as scribe, focusing and refining the class composition.
6. Children write independently.
7. Review and publish.

Most of the writing workshops described focus on developing aspects of writing. Every so often the children need the experience of writing whole stories as well as scenes. This will need extra time. When planning it is important to set aside enough time for a comprehensive unit of work on a particular type of narrative. A block of four or five weeks would provide plenty of time for the children to read many examples of the genre and to develop their understanding and writing skills through the writing workshops, as well as sensibly linking any sentence level features into the writing. All this can involve two or three attempts at a full-blown tale.

It is helpful when planning to begin by deciding the 'big objective', e.g. 'I have Year 4s and by the end of this block of work most of them will be able to write an exciting adventure story at about Level 3 or above.' Starting with the big objective means that the workshops can all relate to the main purpose of the teaching. Planning needs also to take account of the quality of the composition and what aspects have to be taught for the children to improve as writers.

Planning should also involve thinking about different creative ways of enhancing the creation of the children's writing – for instance, opportunities for drama or artwork can help to enhance narrative. Visits to locations may help provide a setting. The sudden discovery of a fragment of a map may act as an exciting spur to the imagination.

Creating the writing mood

At the start of a writing session the atmosphere can draw the children into a creative mood. Many writers cannot begin until the circumstances are right. George Macbeth liked to write with his feet up on a cushion. Bernard Ashley uses a special fountain pen and a hardback book. He writes on one side of the page, leaving the facing page free for alterations. Michael Morpurgo says, 'I do most of my writing in bed – well, on the bed really.' Some need music, others cannot begin without a cup of coffee. What seems to be true is that many writers need a routine to settle into the writing mood.

In school the children have no option as the teacher sets the mood. For the writing to have a hope of containing that elusive, creative spark there may well be certain preconditions, such as:

- the classroom has to be quiet;
- no-one should spoil the atmosphere by mucking about;
- everyone takes it seriously;
- the teacher uses her voice, movements and eyes to draw the children into the spell.

'I have got to write in silence or my characters and world just become ink on a page and I don't find magic in them.' (Jolie, 11 years)

Many children like a very quiet background of music to help them write, for example Mozart or Mahler – something gentle can help. Anthony, 11 years, expresses the views of many children: 'I need quiet to write best, but sometimes conversation and music around me gives me ideas. I can write nearly anywhere if the particular place gives me the right feeling.' But lulling the class will not work on its own! Finding writing ideas that will surprise or intrigue helps – so that the children are on the edge of their seats, wondering what writing task will come their way.

Warming up the word

Many effective teachers of writing begin sessions by playing quick-fire imaginative games. These are intended to limber up the mind. The brain is a muscle – maybe it needs a warm-up by playing linguistic gymnastics. These games help to develop the ability to:

- think swiftly;
- generate words and ideas.

Effective games exercise and strengthen the imagination and could include the following:

- Word association. Give children one minute to write as many words or phrases as possible. Call out a starting point such as *snow, flame, storm, sea*. They have to list as many words as possible – it helps if they try to picture the subject in their minds.
- Rapid writing. Give a time limit of three minutes. The children have to write rapidly about a subject, e.g. *the moon, night, traffic jams, lightning*.
- Crazy writing. Give five minutes to write crazy lists where anything goes, e.g. *I wish I was a lion flying through the breeze, I wish I was a cricket flexing its violin knees, I wish I was an elephant blowing its trumpet*.
- Listing statements. Take a subject and write down in two minutes five statements, e.g. *The moon is a wrinkled face, The moon is a silver silence*.
- Asking questions. Write down five questions you might ask a subject, e.g. *Moon, where are your shoes? Moon, why do you keep so still?*
- Making exclamations. Write a list of exclamations, e.g. *Help me moon! Moon you are a liar!*
- Commands. Boss the subject about, e.g. *Moon, get out of the sky at once! Moon, get washed – we are late*.
- Odd words. From a list of nouns select two that do not seem to go together, e.g. *horse* and *pumpkin*. The children have a few minutes to begin a narrative linking the horse and pumpkin.
- What if. Allow a few minutes for quick writing about 'what would happen if...', e.g. *pencils could talk, trees could walk, dogs flew*.
- The question game. Ask a series of questions that the children have to answer. This could be oral or written speedily, e.g. *Who is there? Where are they? What are they doing? What else is there? What does everyone else think? What happens?*

When playing such games it is important to develop a sense of urgency, to focus the children's intelligence. It does not matter so much what they write – you are looking for them to write fluently, to tap into a writing flow. There are no wrong answers. This is about limbering up the mind. And changing the mind may make writing happen.

Using writing for quick-fire tasks can be helpful, especially as most children enjoy the lack of permanency that a whiteboard offers. If it is wrong – then it can be obliterated! This helps children to write in a more daring fashion as it can remove fear of failure.

Are children unimaginative?

Philip Pullman is quite right when he says that if you do not want to read, then you are unlikely to be someone who wants to write. For writing stems from reading. Natalie, 11 years, comments that 'I like to read other people's work because I sometimes get ideas from them. I get my best ideas from thinking what I want to say, but change the words so that they sound right and make sense.' The problem for many children is not a lack of imagination. If I sit down to write a story then I am already half-way there – my mind is crammed with possibilities: kings, queens, boy wizards, burly thieves, lonely towers, windswept marshes, busy city centres, abandoned children, invisibility rings... I have read so much that my mind is already full of the basic building blocks. I just have to plunder this resource. If children have not read, then they lack this storehouse of possibilities garnered from reading. They may be just as imaginative as Tolstoy – but without reading they will have little clue how a story might run.

Waiting for inspiration

'Inspiration is what people who don't write wait for,' says Jan Mark. Careful planning, using experience, and letting the imagination wonder what might happen, is the writer's stock in trade. Of course, the odd moment of inspiration will poke its head in. For instance, when I cracked open a walnut one Year 6 lad shouted out, 'It's like a brain!' This has changed the way I see walnuts. Whenever I have one now I cannot help but think that I am a cannibal, eating a miniature brain. These moments of inspiration, images and ideas just pop from nowhere into the mind. But for that to happen, the intensity, the concentration, the writing mood has to be there. The imagination has to be trained so that it can concentrate, and create the new from the known. A weak imagination will not be able to follow the possibilities and invent.

Trapping ideas

Children should not settle down to write unless they have already generated ideas for their writing. The use of a writing journal will provide a seedbed of possibilities that can be used. Indeed, for many writers the act of sifting is important. Theresa Breslin says, 'I never have to look for ideas. They stick themselves under my nose! My problem is that I have far too many ideas, boxes of notes, wee cuttings out of newspapers.' Peter Redgrove, the poet, suggests too that 'the world is full of creative suggestions: it is composed of them... take up these ideas... they are found in chance observations, words overheard, sudden headlines, fragments of dreams... set down these hints and guesses, sudden clarifications, brief mysteries, unexpected openings.' Techniques for generating ideas and for organising them can be introduced and taught, including:

- listing what we know;
- brainstorming words and ideas;
- listing the main points;
- organising ideas into a structure – such as a flow chart or paragraph plan.

Some children struggle with writing narrative because they have not internalised a range of possible structures. So their writing aimlessly rambles. This can be helped by:

- retelling known stories;
- innovating on known stories by altering the characters, setting or events but keeping a familiar structure.

Plenty of imitation and innovation helps to strengthen the imaginative storehouse of possibilities. Once children have sufficient narrative experiences they can begin to invent their own tales, simply by manoeuvring their characters into settings, providing experiences, and dilemmas to resolve. The writer becomes like the grand chess master manipulating the flow of the tale, mingling many tales to create something new.

Writers get ideas from:

- observation – looking directly at an object or experience. Ted Hughes actually stood outside a jaguar's cage, notebook in hand, watching it pace up and down. Sally, 9 years, told me that poetry was 'when you say what things are really like.'
- memory quest – using details from a memory.

'Sometimes stories begin with real situations but after that I take off into the unknown.' (Jenny Nimmo)

- brainstorm – rapidly jotting down any word, phrases or ideas that spring to mind. 'Some of my best ideas come from my imagination. If an idea appears in my head I quickly jot it down.' (Alison, 11 years)
- daydreaming ideas, what might happen. 'What I like best is what I call "dream time" – thinking about a story, weaving it in my head.' (Michael Morpurgo) 'I get ideas from things out of this world which squeeze out from the back of my head.' (Kerry, 10 years)
- visualising – picturing in the mind what you are writing about. 'I get ideas when the room is deep in thought. Sometimes looking out of the window helps to bring pictures to my mind.' (Mark, 10 years)
- telling before writing.
- letting the mind roam – wondering.
- notes in their writing journal – checking back.
- things they have read, heard or seen. 'Ideas come from photos, questions I want answered, overheard snippets of conversations, daydreams.' (Michelle Magorian)

Igniting the writing

Story writers need:

- a plot with possibilities;
- characters to make the plot happen;
- a believable setting.

Teachers can ignite writing by seeking different ways to entrance the child's imagination. This may be as simple as passing round a rusty key or a golden ring as a starting point. Teacher demonstration and shared writing are vital strategies for helping children see the different possibilities and to teach children how to improve their own writing. Just before writing, reading aloud examples helps to set the atmosphere and provides a yardstick. The rhythm of the sentences should echo on the writer's mind. Once the children are ready to write, a swift transition into the act of composition is needed – too often the spell can be lost.

During writing

Most writers have a special place for their writing. They have to be comfortable and often like to surround themselves with knick-knacks. Whilst this may not suit the classroom environment, there are a few secrets to writing that need to be thought about:

- concentrate hard as you write – let nothing else intrude, ignore all interruptions;
- speed – write quickly, so speedily that there is barely time to think;
- rehearse – mutter away the sentences as you write. 'I always speak the dialogue aloud to see if it sounds right.' (Jill Murphy) 'I go through the drafts in my mind first.' (Miroslav Holub)
- reread – keep rereading so that sentences flow on from each other;
- picture – see what you are writing about in your mind's eye;
- tell it – listen to the inner voice telling the tale. 'I write because I enjoy making things happen to me, creating pictures which nobody else can see unless they read my stories.' (Jolene, 11 years)

Finding fictional space

There is a 'fictional space' that writers enter. It is like a trance. In the same way that a reader is transported into a secondary world where the mind's eye sees the story unfold, so too the writer has to enter a fictional space to follow the inner voice, to see the story unfold, to chase the words across the page. Many of us can recall those moments when, as a child, we were writing a story so quickly that the wrist ached. It was almost as if there is a voice in the head telling the story, and the writer is trying to keep up with it – this is the 'story-teller' in the head and writers have to train themselves to listen in to that inner voice.

Grammar for imagination

The more automatic the basics of writing the less they interfere with composition. To put it bluntly, if the child is worried about handwriting, spelling or where to put the full stop then the composition will lack flow. These things have to become second nature. Children need to be so skilful at choosing words and constructing sentences that this does not delay the act of writing in any way. In the same way, the teaching of grammar has to focus not on endless exercises (which probably slow progress in writing) but on how to use words, construct and vary sentences and make texts cohere. Grammar should be taught so that the imagination can be fully used.

After writing

Some writers like to put their work away and revisit it after a while. In this way they return to it more as a reader, rather than the writer. This helps them to shape, polish and improve. Children should be used to always reading their writing aloud to a partner or group. Usually this helps the writer to hear or see where the words need improving or the text is clumsy. The end of the trail should be publishing stories, poems and non-fiction in books, magazines, anthologies, on tape or as a performance for others. Providing a genuine audience puts language under pressure – the writer will want to get it right!

Writing as a serious game

In many ways writing is like play. It is a serious game, where the writer creates new worlds, helping the reader to step into another dimension. Writers know that they can do it. Children do not. This is why they have to be treated as writers – so that the self-image is strong. The teacher must also become a writer. Every good teacher of writing I have met writes with, and in front of the children, sometimes sharing their own attempts. Ted Hughes sums up the conditions for writing succinctly: 'by showing to a pupil's imagination many opportunities and few restraints, and instilling into him confidence and a natural motive for writing, the odds are that something – maybe not much, but something – of our common genius will begin to put a word in.'

Capturing stories

Planning or discovering?

Writers approach planning in different ways. It is as if they are on a continuum, with planners at one extreme and discoverers at the other.

Planners like to jot down every detail. P. G. Wodehouse knew exactly what was going to happen in great detail. He planned paragraphs, even thinking up the jokes! This meant that by the time he came to write, the book was almost written and would need little revision. Philip Pullman says that he never writes a first draft. He always aims to write a final draft! For young writers, too much planning may kill the desire to write.

Discoverers like to launch in and see where the story takes them. They discover the tale as they go along. The problem with this approach is that it may involve wasting time going in a fruitless direction and often leads to many revisions, so that for these writers their stories do not get written but rewritten! For young writers, whilst launching in may be exciting, unless they have internalised a strong sense of structure the likelihood is that their story will ramble with inconsequential scenes. Too much revision can become tedious and turn children off!

Writers lean one way or another. Nico, aged 7, said to me that he liked stories because 'you never know what's going to happen'. He enjoyed the sense of discovery through the act of writing. To some extent he wouldn't want to know what happens, in the same way that knowing the end of a good story can spoil it for the reader.

The answer perhaps lies in ensuring that young writers start writing once they are well prepared. It is helpful to have sorted out a basic idea and built up a background to the story. A simple structure can leave sufficient room for new scenes and ideas to be used, but will also provide enough structure to hold the tale together.

Knowing an ending is important. This is because narrative drives towards the problem and then on towards the resolution. With no ending in sight the tale may meander hopelessly. Young writers should work towards an ending but bear in mind that if a better idea crops up, as they near the ending, this may be worth pursuing. The key is to end with a well-shaped story, which does not include rambling events that slow the tale down and bear no real relation to the forwards movement of the plot.

Writing tips

- Knowing where you think you are going may mean that you are less likely to ramble or lose your way. But do not be afraid of moving away from the plan if something better comes along.
- Don't plan too rigidly or the story may sound false. Many writers find that once they get going, the story begins to tell itself. Sometimes you are writing so quickly that your wrist aches – and you can hear a voice in your head telling the story, and there you are trying to keep up. This helps the writing flow. So, allow yourself to make discoveries and be surprised (and have fun) as you travel along.

Seven ways to capture and structure plots

On the following pages are a small number of common strategies used by writers for planning a simple outline of their plot. Some lend themselves naturally to certain stories, e.g. journey stories, such as *The Hobbit*, lend themselves to story maps. Select with the class a planning technique to use before writing. When only a paragraph is being written little planning is needed. It may be sufficient to talk through the structure of the paragraph or list what might happen, e.g. *character enters room, crosses room and leaves*.

1. Draw a map of the events (Figure 1).

Figure 1 Story map for 'Adventure of Mr Fox'

2. Use a time line to plot (Figure 2).

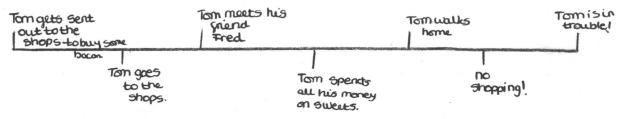

Figure 2 Time line for a 'forgetting' story

3. Fill in scenes on Post-its and move them around (Figure 3).

These scenes can be moved round to provide a dramatic opening plus a flashback.

Figure 3 Moving scenes

4. List scenes and jot on connectives (Figure 4).

Scenes	Scene Starters.
1. Mr twit buys an Elephant for his wife's birthday.	.Early one morning . . . . .
2. He takes it home.	First of all, he takes it home.
3. He hides the Elephant.	Mr. Twit had to hide the elephant·· ··
4. He goes down to the garden.	After that he went. . . . .
5. Mrs. Twit finds the Elephant.	"What on Earth is that!"··
6. She takes it back to the zoo.	So that afternoon···· .
7. She swaps it for a lion.	"I like the look of that..!!
8. She takes it home and hides it instead of the Elephant.	As soon as she had paid for the lion she hid it.
9. Mr. twit finds it!	. At that moment the lion lept out onto Mr. Twit.

Figure 4 Scene list for a story based on a Roald Dahl character

5. Draw a storyboard (Figure 5).

Figure 5 Storyboard 'Eddie and the puddle'

6. Write a flow chart (Figure 6).

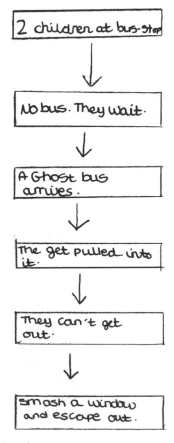

Figure 6 Flow chart for a 'Ghost bus'

7. Create a simple paragraph grid (Figure 7).

• Anne and Tom decide to go shopping at the new Centre in town. To get a birthday Presents for their best friends Sally and Alexendra.	• They meet up at Tom's house and, together get enough money to afford two train tickets into the town Centre. which is three hours away from where they live.	• They walk to the nearest train Station and buy their tickets. They wait for the train to come but in the end they go to check the time on the board. As the train hasn't come yet.	• Tom reads the wrong time the train goes, and they miss their train. They Start to Panic as they is not another train back home to where they live.
• They try ringing their parents up. But there is no answer! Anne starts to get angry and fustrated with tom and there is a arguement between them.	• It starts to get dark and cold and hardly anyone is around. Anne tries to ask people if they know where you can get a taxi but no-one knows.	• Anne remembers that her untie lives nearby and they walk to her house. She is there and looks after them.	• Anne's mum comes and takes them home. But they realise they don't have a birthday Present. But luckily Anne's mum got one for them!

Figure 7 Paragraph grid for 'The mistake'

Introduction to four basic workshops

The following four workshops provide strategies to select from that will help to develop the skill of planning and preparing before writing. These are approaches that will be used again and again, whenever children settle down to write whole stories.

● Basic workshop 1 – this provides ideas for generating a few possibilities, getting going.
● Basic workshop 2 – this workshop builds on workshop 1, in that it focuses upon helping children decide on the basic plot idea and a trigger to get the tale going.
● Basic workshop 3 – this workshop provides ideas for basing the plot upon a known tale.
● Basic workshop 4 – this workshop provides a few common story types that might be used or adapted to help provide structure.

Basic workshop 1 – techniques for creating story ideas

The ideas in this workshop can be used in many different ways and on many occasions. These are basic strategies for creating story ideas. Many children find writing narrative difficult because they have no story to tell. They do need to internalise a basic sense of the shape of narrative, and to have picked up a number of basic structures for writing stories.

Ask the class where they think writers get their ideas. Discuss the notion that writers are like thieves. They plunder each other's writing, often sparking new ideas from old stories – as well as raiding their own lives. Writers are constantly on the lookout for ideas – in everyday events, things they read, see on TV, hear on the radio. Here are a number of linked techniques that writers use.

Keeping a running list of ideas

Keep a running list of possible ideas for stories. This could be kept on several pages in a writing journal or on a wall poster. When a child (or the class) gets a new idea, they make a note of it.

Brainstorming ideas

Brainstorm ideas as a class or group, or individually. This consists of spending a short period of time just firing out possible ideas – rapidly jotting down any word, phrases, or ideas that spring to mind (Figure 8). 'Some of my best ideas come from my imagination. If an idea appears in my head I quickly jot it down.' (Alison, 11 years)

Useful starting points are:

supposing...
what if...
wishes
lies
secrets
dreams
unusual people
secret places
fears
problems

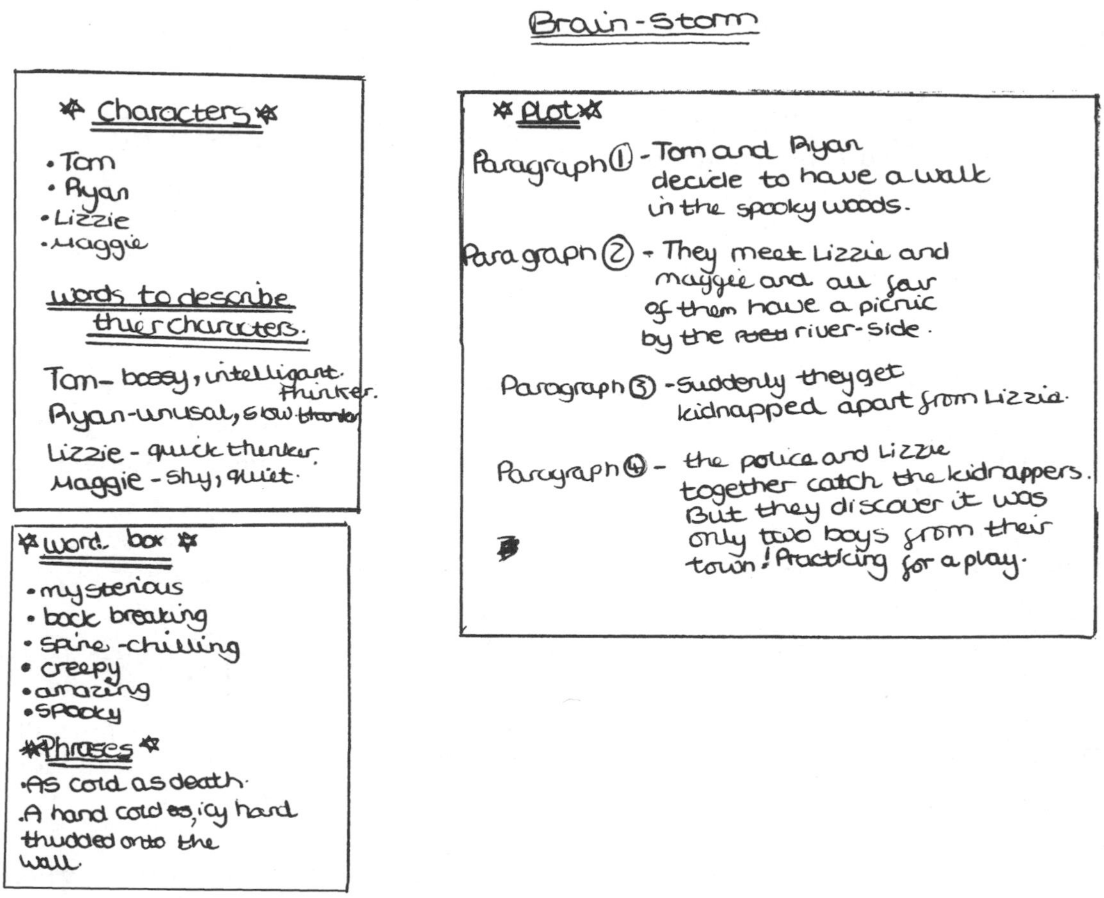

Brain-Storm

Characters

• Tom
• Ryan
• Lizzie
• Maggie

words to describe thier characters.

Tom- bossy, intelligant, thinker.
Ryan- unusal, slow thinker
Lizzie - quick thinker.
Maggie - shy, quiet.

word box

• mysterious
• back breaking
• spine -chilling
• creepy
• amazing
• spooky

Phrases
• As cold as death.
• A hand cold es, icy hand thudded onto the wall

Plot

Paragraph ① - Tom and Ryan decide to have a walk in the spooky woods.

Paragraph ② - They meet Lizzie and maggie and all four of them have a picnic by the river-side.

Paragraph ③ -Suddenly they get kidnapped apart from Lizzie.

Paragraph ④ - the police and Lizzie together catch the kidnappers. But they discover it was only two boys from their town! Practicing for a play.

Figure 8 Organised brainstorm

Engaging in a memory quest

Use details from the memory. 'Sometimes stories begin with real situations but after that I take off into the unknown.' (Jenny Nimmo)

Sometimes the best stories come from taking something that has happened. This may well be a simple tale of the family huffing and puffing their way up a hill at the weekend! The idea is for the children to take a family 'story' and fictionalise it, giving the people different names and possibly throwing in some extra invented scenes. Keep it simple and clear. Possible starting points could include:

strange places
a frightening person
my worst memory
grandpa/grandma
frightening events

a row
a funny thing that happened
getting lost
getting hurt
being frightened
getting caught out
crazes
running away
breaking something
stealing
tricks
April Fool
moving school/house
making new friends
breaking friends
my best place
my best holiday

Setting aside daydreaming time

Many writers spend time daydreaming their ideas, wondering what might happen. It can help if you give the class an idea of what they will be writing about a week in advance. Remind them every day. Very often, by the time the allotted day for writing has arrived, many children will have already sorted out their basic plot – the subconscious will have got itself prepared. A tale will be found, mulled over and shaped.

'What I like best is what I call "dream time" – thinking about a story, weaving it in my head.' (Michael Morpurgo)

'I get ideas from things out of this world which squeeze out from the back of my head.' (Kerry, 10 years)

Visualising ideas

One useful tactic is for the class to close their eyes and try to see or imagine a story. In their minds, they try to picture what they will be writing about. You may need to talk them through a starting point. You might begin in one of three ways.

1. **A person** – the story begins with a character. The character is standing in the street. Think about what this person looks like. It might be someone you know or have seen before. How are they feeling? Where are they about to go? What is this person about to do?
2. **A place** – the story begins with a place. Where is this place? It is probably somewhere that you have been. Are there houses? Is this place in the countryside or the town? What time of day is it? What is the weather like? What is there in your place that is interesting? Has someone left

something or hidden something there? What is about to happen? Who is about to come on to the scene?
3. **An event** – the story begins with an event, something happening. What is going on? Is someone happy and laughing or are they crying? Is someone angry and shouting? Has someone done something wrong or is someone creeping along about to do something?

Part of the skill is talking the class into a story – keep your questions and prompts general and you will find that different children get their own ideas. Playing music, such as Mozart, can help stimulate visualising. 'I get ideas when the room is deep in thought. Sometimes looking out of the window helps to bring pictures to my mind.' (Mark, 10 years)

Having starting points

There are a number of useful starting points that can trigger a story idea. Having an eye for something intriguing or a little out of the ordinary can help to generate thinking. Here are some possible starting points:

- **Objects** – an old key, a coil of rope, a bell, an ornate box, a pair of glasses, a watch...
- **Postcards** – postcards of scenes do not work so well as postcards of paintings; collect striking pictures of people, group scenes, unusual places...anything that seems to offer possibilities....
- **Posters** – large posters of scenes, people or events can act as good whole-class prompts...
- **Video clips** – short clips of people, places or events can help to begin a tale and form the basis for writing extensions...
- **Locations** – take the class out to a nearby location: an old church, a deserted house, the corner of the street, the allotments...
- **People** – strange people we have met, funny relatives, pictures of people....
- **Messages** – a phone call, a letter, a telegram, a secret message torn in half...
- **Powerful symbols** – a tower, a mirror, a pond, a door, a window...

You will need to ask a few questions. For example: Whose is this? Where was it found? What does it do? Why is it precious? How did it get there? Who is coming to pick it up? What is going to happen next?

Mind-mapping

Mind-mapping is rather like brainstorming. You will need to do this a number of times as a whole class. However, once the children get the idea, they can create their own mind maps on whiteboards or on large sheets of paper. The idea is to create a map of possible thoughts (Figure 9). Some of these can be elaborated or added to, in order to embellish them. It is essential that the teacher leads the children in the mapping when they are inexperienced. This is done with a series of questions. Bear in mind that you need to generate a few essentials for any mind-mapping sessions:

● some possible settings
● a girl and a boy of about the same age as the class
● a possible event or trigger to get the story going.

It can help to start with an object which is written in the centre of the map (an old key, a lamp, a letter, a ring, etc.). Now start building up a picture, rapidly, by asking questions. For example: Tell me about this ring. Who owns the ring? What's her name? How old is she? Where does she live? She has two children – about your age. What is the girl called? How old is she? Where is she? How is she feeling? What about the boy? What is he called? Where is he? Why is he there? What is he doing? How is he feeling? Why?

Jot down the responses around the board, clustering those that go together. Remember to build up a collection of possibilities around both the boy and the girl. Useful prompts include: What is wrong? What might happen next? How do they feel? What is unusual about this place? There is something secret hidden nearby... One of them has lost/found something that is precious... One of them is afraid of something...One of these children has a great wish... One has told a lie/done something wrong... A stranger is about to visit them...

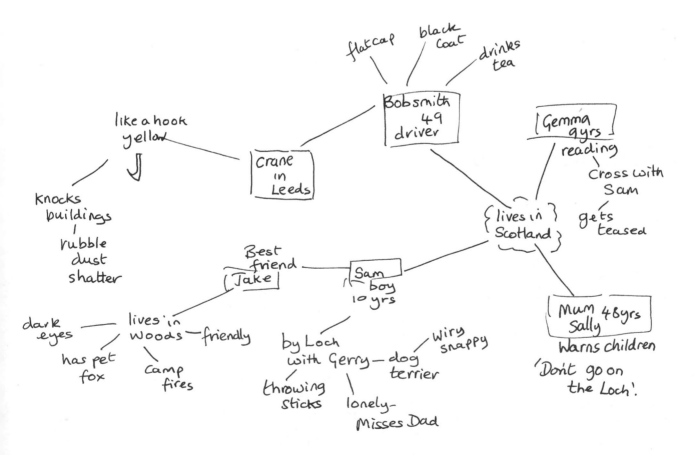

Figure 9 Mind map

Telling before writing

Very often we rush children into writing when they haven't sufficiently captured a story. Spend a few minutes with children, working in pairs or threes, to give them the opportunity to tell their story before writing. In this way they can rehearse the basic plot idea, getting it clear in their minds.

Spending some time in generating a story will be useful in the long run. Adult writers tend to spend quite a lot of time mulling over story ideas, researching the background, mapping out possibilities, getting to know their characters. You might find it helpful to combine some of the suggested techniques above. Remember to keep this introductory work lively, swift and intense. It should stimulate and set the mind buzzing with narrative possibilities – not become dull and ponderous!

✍ Writing tips

- Going in cold is not advisable. Children should become familiar with using brainstorming and mind-mapping, in order to help them enter their story world and explore possibilities. This means they can begin writing with various avenues open, loaded with some provisions for the story journey.
- Children need to know that stories do not have to be completely invented. They can work from what they know and can see, and add in some invention. Most writers use bits of people and places they know. This helps to make the story seem real.

Basic workshop 2 – creating story triggers and plot ideas

Plot ideas

It is helpful to have some sort of basic plot idea. This may well have been generated by brainstorming, mind-mapping, or looking at an object. The plot idea can usually be explained in one or two sentences and needs to be quite simple, e.g. 'Two children get lost by the canal but in the end find their way home.'

The plot idea needs to explain the dilemma (what goes wrong) and the resolution (how it gets sorted out). A simple starting point is for the children to express a well-known story as a simple plot idea. For example:

- 'Cinderella' – A girl is not allowed to go to a ball, but is helped by a fairy godmother and ends up marrying a prince.
- 'Red Riding Hood' – A girl takes provisions to her grandmother, who has been eaten by a wolf. The grandmother and the girl are saved by a woodcutter.
- 'Humpty Dumpty' – An egg falls off a wall and cannot be mended.
- 'Three Little Pigs' – Three pigs nearly get eaten by a wolf, but they get even in the end.

Move on to longer stories, but make sure that the plot idea is kept to the bare minimum. For example:

- *James and the Giant Peach* – A lonely boy travels to America in a magic peach and makes new friends.
- *Flat Stanley* – A boy becomes squashed flat, but has many adventures.
- *Harry Potter* – Harry goes to a school for wizards and manages to overcome an evil enemy.

Putting the story into a few simple sentences helps to encapsulate the basic idea.

Story triggers

If the children are beginning their story with a character or a place then they may well need a trigger to get the story going. This can be a small event that just sets the narrative in motion. Brainstorm various possibilities by placing the character in a setting and then asking: something suddenly happens – what might that be? It doesn't have to be dramatic. For example:

- an ice cream van comes down the road;
- a dog comes bounding over;
- an old man falls over;
- the phone rings;
- someone's mum starts shouting;
- a car screeches round the corner;
- it starts raining;
- the main character sees a pound coin on the ground.

Practise using the trigger to set the story in motion. This could be limited to a simple paragraph. Begin by demonstrating one idea from the list:

As the rain began to fall, Sasha huddled in a shop doorway. The smells of the chip shop next door drifted past her, making her more hungry than ever.

Her attention was caught by an old man making his way slowly, and with great care, taking one footstep at a time down the pavement towards her. His eyes were scrunched up against the driving rain. She watched, unable to help as he slipped and almost in slow motion stumbled into the road. There was a screech of brakes.

Then write one together as a class before they write individually.

Provide the opening few words to a paragraph for the children to use.

> Ty sat on the park bench.
> The beach was quite empty now.
> By the time Dad got home, the two girls had already started.
> Stalker waited by the cinema door.
> That evening, crouched behind the wall, they waited.
> Sal stuck her head out from between the coats.
> Belle let out an almighty whoop and ran.
> The sea pounded the cliffs below.

✏️ Writing tips

- It does help if children keep their story ideas simple. Some children over-complicate their writing, try to write *War and Peace*, and run the risk of becoming muddled or losing heart.
- It is worth noting that some writers plan a basic framework to guide their writing – whereas some like to work from a basic plot idea, e.g. two children get lost on the moors but find their way home in the end. Once a basic idea is born, the children may need to structure their thinking by using a flow chart, storyboard, or paragraph grid or by jotting down a list of scenes.

Basic workshop 3 – stealing plots from known stories

It is probably true to say that there are only a few basic stories – and all writers are playing about with the same basic plots. Explore with the class the most basic shape of story:

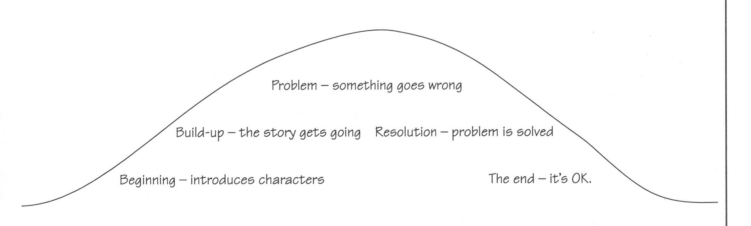

Of course, many plots look more like a mountain range. A TV soap series would look like this:

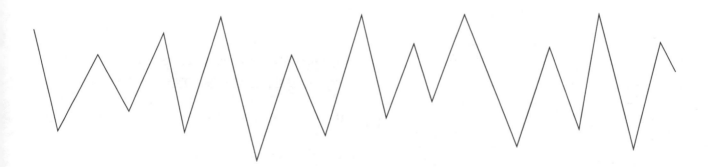

Some simple plots can be created by basing ideas on well-known tales and extracting the underlying principle. Fairy tales, myths, legends and jokes can be used in this way.

To run a workshop in this vein you will need to select your story, using a fairy tale or simple picture book, and then follow this basic routine.

1. Read the tale.
2. Extract the basic plot.
3. Then translate this into general terms.
4. Take this skeleton and bring it alive (e.g. by changing the characters or setting but keeping to the basic plot structure).

Use 'Red Riding Hood' as a simple example.

1. **Read the tale.** Begin by reading the story through – a simple version meant for younger children would do.
2. **Extract the basic plot.** To extract the basic plot ask the children to write down the main scenes on Post-its or small cards. Working individually, they should list up to eight main events and then, working in twos and threes, they should match their ideas and place them in order. They must discard minor scenes and just focus on the main events. (A main event might be described as being an event that the story cannot do without – i.e. if it is taken out, the storyline collapses!) As a class, agree together on the key scenes – write these up on the board, using boxes to section off each scene.

> a) RR is asked to take provisions to grandma.

> b) RR walks through the forest.

> c) She meets a woodcutter who asks where she is going.

> d) A wolf overhears the conversation and races ahead to the cottage.

> e) The wolf eats grandma and disguises himself as her.

> f) RR arrives and is taken in by the wolf.

> g) The wolf is about to kill RR.

> h) The woodcutter arrives and kills the wolf.

3. **Then translate this into general terms**.

> a) The main character is asked to run an errand.

> b) The main character sets off.

> c) The main character meets someone friendly who directs them.

> d) An unpleasant person overhears the conversation and races ahead of the main character.

> e) The unpleasant person waits at the destination.

> f) The main character arrives and is fooled by the unpleasant person.

> g) The unpleasant person threatens the main character.

> h) The friendly character arrives in the nick of time and overpowers the unpleasant person.

4. **Take this skeleton and bring it alive.**

"Jo," yelled Mrs Petrus, her hands numb with pain. "Take this stuff round to old Mrs Carter at number 38 will you?" There was a grunt from the sitting room. And Mrs Petrus massaged her hands together. They were bad today. It was always bad when it rained.

At that moment Jo poked her head round the kitchen door, grabbed the bag and shot out, without even a word. Her mother shook her head, switched on the portable TV and settled back to watch Coronation Street.

✐ Writing tip

- Use the basic underlying pattern of simple, well-known tales to provide a skeleton structure for the children's own writing.

Basic workshop 4 – using common story types

Many writers have tussled with the idea that there are only a few basic story forms. This workshop introduces a number of basic plots. You could recycle these plots by changing the settings, characters, or time; adding in different events; or using flashbacks to alter the order of scenes.

When reading stories, encourage the children to decide the 'type' that they are looking at – many stories will be variants of those listed below. Working with a few simple patterns can liberate some writers, as they no longer have to tussle with what is going to happen – the map of events is already understood. This can free up thinking space, so that the brain has more room to focus upon the quality of the writing. Basic patterns include the following.

The wishing tale

Many stories are built around our natural desire to have something – whether that is love, money, power, or just a Gameboy or a pair of trainers! The wishing tale's basic structure looks like this:

1. The main character wants something badly.
2. The main character tries to get it.
3. The main character is prevented by some sort of difficulty.
4. The main character overcomes the difficulty.
5. The main character gets what they want.
6. The end – was it worth it?

A popular variation on this story is to begin at the point when the main character has just got whatever they wanted. Ask the children the following questions (typical responses are in brackets):

1. Who is your main character? (Joe, Rebecca, etc.)
2. What have they just been given? (Gameboy, trainers, a camera, etc.)
3. Who paid for it? (Mum or Dad.)
4. Could they afford it? (No.)
5. What happens to it? (It gets trashed, broken, nicked, etc.)

The basic frame for the story could run as follows:

1. The main character has just got a precious item from an adult/friend.
2. The item gets stolen, broken, lost or destroyed.
3. The main character has to retrieve or renew the item.
4. The main character tries hard to do this.
5. At long last, the main character succeeds.
6. The adult/friend finds out and comments.

An exclamation opening would be useful for this sort of tale. For example:

A new pair of trainers! At long last! I stared at them, bulging off my feet as I stomped around the kitchen . . .

In the fairy tale version of the wishing tale the main character is granted three wishes but uses them unwisely and ends up with no advantage. This simple pattern might be imitated by replacing the idea of a magic wish with a stroke of luck:

1. The main character performs a good deed by helping someone out.
2. The main character has a remarkable stroke of luck.
3. The main character enjoys whatever luck brought.
4. Something goes wrong and luck runs out.
5. The main character is back to square one – but may have made a friend.

The warning tale

Many good stories are built around a basic warning. Roald Dahl's book *The Minpins* is built around the mother's warning to the main character, Billy, that he should not go over the road into the forest. Michael Morpurgo's *Why the Whales Came* begins with the warning that the children should not play with the Birdman . . .

Children are always being told what they cannot do – and so this theme appeals. I often begin by asking them to make a list of warnings, applicable to school and home. ('What are you told that you mustn't do?') The list is often quite lengthy! Usually many of the ideas would lend themselves to a simple story about what happens when you do what you have been warned against. The story frame might run like this:

1. The two main characters are warned not to do something.
2. They set off.
3. They get tempted. (One may be reluctant but gets dragged along.)
4. They do what they have been warned against.
5. Something goes wrong and they are in deep trouble.
6. One gets free and goes for help.
7. The other waits, desperately.
8. They are rescued – and told off for breaking the warning!

The warning tale opens effectively with the actual warning. For example:

"Don't go to the dump. It's dangerous," snapped Mr Jones, lowering his glasses and looking at the two boys.

"Of course not, Dad," muttered Chas. But his fingers were crossed behind his back . . .

The losing tale

This story hinges around the common human theme of loss. The main character loses something of value and has to either find it or replace it in some way:

1. The main character is given something.
2. The main character goes off.
3. The main character has a good time.
4. The main character realises they have lost what they were given.
5. The main character vainly searches for the lost item.
6. The main character goes home/school to face the music.
7. The main character finds the item in an unexpected place.

The finding tale

This story is built around the idea of finding something that looks good but turns out to be worthless or dangerous in some way:

1. The main character goes somewhere.
2. The main character starts doing something.
3. The main character finds something unusual, amazing, important.
4. Something goes wrong.
5. It is the fault of the object they found.
6. The main character has to put it back/return it to the owner/hide it/throw it away.

The tale of quest

Many stories are built around the notion of a quest, from *Rosie's Walk* to *The Hobbit*! The basic idea is to send the characters on a journey from *a* to *b*. Somewhere along the line, they have to overcome various hurdles. These can be small scenes or whole chapters. Of course, life is a form of journey, complete with its own hurdles. Looked at in this way, many stories fall into this category. The story frame might run like this:

1. The main character sets off on a journey.
2. Something small goes wrong.
3. Something worse happens.
4. Something even worse happens.
5. The main character gets there in the end.

The tale of defeating the monster

At its simplest level, this is the story of Jack. It has a basic four-part structure. Each part could consist of many paragraphs or chapters:

1. All is well.
2. But a giant comes along.
3. The giant wreaks havoc.
4. Jack kills it!

Many stories and films are built around this idea – if the concept of the monster is stretched to include a terrible disease, a hurricane, unemployment, death in a family, a bully, a horrible teacher. The monster is anything that upsets the status quo. To write this sort of story, the children need to begin by deciding where their characters are. The opening must establish that all is well and everyone is happy. The build-up needs to create the picture of the characters having a good time. Then the 'monster' or problem is introduced, followed by what happens as a result. The tale must show how the characters' lives change for the worse. However, the characters have to overcome the monster in some way, so that by the end all is well. Again this is the basic shape of our lives – a constant struggle against 'monsters' that rear up to disturb the equilibrium we try to create.

The meeting tale

This is built around the basic notion of what happens when people meet. It helps if children build up two contrasting characters. They then need to think about where they will meet. What are they both doing there? A simple pattern based on this idea might look as follows:

1. Two characters meet.
2. They disagree.
3. They go their separate ways.
4. Something happens to one of them.
5. The other saves them.
6. They agree!

The key to this type of tale is to use contrasting characters.

The tale of fear

It is useful to spend time working out simple structures with the class. For example:

1. The main character is afraid of something.
2. The main character gets teased about this.
3. The main character sets off.
4. What they fear happens.
5. The main character manages to get through it.
6. All is OK – the main character has conquered their fear.

Encourage them to think through what might happen next. Keep the structure simple. In this way they internalise a sense of structure and will get used to building simple text patterns. Less confident writers may take each section and turn it into a paragraph. More mature writers may well write several paragraphs for each section; they may also want to move parts of the story around. For instance they could start with the dilemma, so that their tale gets off to a punchy beginning, and then use a flashback to take the reader back to the preceding events. It helps to see each section as a scene that can be moved about.

✏ Writing tips

- Get the children to use a basic working title right from the start – even if they think they might change it.
- It can help to number pages, space out writing so that it can be seen, and leave gaps for possible illustrations – these also help to give a feeling of covering space!
- Children need to see stories as a series of scenes.
- If they get stuck, they should refer back to the basic story frame or imagine the next scene – what might happen next? It can also help to 'see the story' or quickly jot down a few possibilities in their writing journal. The plot can be pushed forward by introducing a new character or making something happen (e.g. of an unexpected nature, such as the discovery of a message or an old letter, or the phone ringing...). When stuck it does help to reread what has been written so far – this may help to spark an idea.
- Have a class poster of triggers and basic plot ideas.
- Try giving out story titles and ideas well before the writing day – so the children can think about their stories, mulling over what might happen.
- Plan long stories in parts, e.g. part one, part two, etc. or chapter one, chapter two, etc. When children move from one part to the next, encourage them to leave a space on the page or begin a new page. Structure their time so that they can build up their story step by step, scene by scene. Quests and journeys make good subjects for extended story-writing.
- Make a class collection of paragraph openings, as these can help to shift a story forwards, e.g. 'Suddenly...' or ' It was a week later that...'

- Remind children that if they know about their character's feelings/problems/flaws at the start of the story, then they can think about what happens to change them.
- Collect dilemmas – problems to solve, mysteries, difficulties to overcome, calamities, dramatic events.
- Often use the simplest story shape – everything all right at the beginning, a build-up of events that leads to a dilemma, then a series of events that lead towards a resolution and ending.
- Use anecdotes and simple everyday events for short stories, e.g. breaking a window.

Characterisation

Objectives:

Y3 T1 Sentence 7, 8: conventions of speech marks; Text 2, 10, 15: how dialogue is presented in stories, e.g. through statements, questions, exclamations; use reading as a model; write own passages of dialogue; use paragraphing to organise dialogue.

Y3 T2 Text 3, 8: identify and discuss main and recurring characters, evaluate their behaviour, and justify views; write portraits of characters.

Y3 T3 Text 5: discuss character's feelings, behaviour, relationships, etc.

Y4 T1 Text 2, 11: identify characteristics of key characters; write character sketches, focusing on details to evoke sympathy or dislike.

Y4 T2 Text 2: understand how settings influence events and affect characters' behaviour.

Y4 T3 Text 11, 12: explore main issues of a story by writing a story about a dilemma and the issues it raises for the character; write an alternative ending for a known story and discuss how this would change the reader's view of the characters.

Y5 T1 Text 3, 15: investigate how characters are presented through dialogue, action, and description, how the reader responds to them, and what their relationships with other characters are like; write new characters into a story.

Y5 T3 Text 7: write from another character's point of view.

Y6 T1 Text 7: plan characters quickly and effectively.

Workshop 1 – planning your character

Write these sentences on the board and ask: Which sentence tells us more about the character? How does the writer manage this?

> She came down the lane.
> Freddie stormed across the London road without looking either way.

Take feedback. The second sentence is more effective as the writer gives us:

- a name (*Freddie*);
- a powerful verb suggesting that Freddie is angry (*stormed*);
- further details suggesting Freddie's anger or single-mindedness (*without looking either way*).

Already the reader is building a mental picture of Freddie as being in a desperate and furious rush – on a mission of some urgency!

In groups, or pairs, children analyse the following example – what strategies does the writer use to help build up the character?

> Coral Ocean stood on the edge of the playground and waited. No one came near. All the other kids seemed to be absorbed in their own games. She gazed out through the railings and pretended to notice something interesting in the distance. Blinking back tears, she roughly rubbed her eyes and hoped that no one would notice.
>
> "What's up?" A tall boy had come across and stood bouncing a tennis ball against the shed.
>
> "Clear off," snapped Coral, not yet ready to even try.
>
> "Keep your hair on," muttered the boy. He spun round and raced back across the playground, bouncing his ball as he went. Coral could see him chatting to some other boys and pointing back at her.

Make a list of the different strategies. For example:

- using an interesting name;
- using powerful verbs to reflect how the character feels;
- using a few details to suggest what the character is like;
- suggesting further what the character is like through use of dialogue and speech verbs;
- giving the thoughts and reactions of others;
- revealing the character's own thoughts and reactions.

Now look at the key aspects in turn.

Names

When planning, the first thing to do is to choose the right name for the main character. The name *Bill* does not do much for me – but *Scrooge* seems to say it all. Notice how writers like Roald Dahl choose names that evoke something about the character. What good names do the children know from their own reading? When writing, it helps to choose names carefully. Ask children to start an ongoing list of 'good names for stories' in their writing journals, e.g. *Freddie Pilcher, Bodger White, Maggot Gibson, Bomber, Petie Fisher, Skater, Mrs Savage*, etc. They should be on the lookout for good names – on billboards, shop fronts, signs, etc.

Special details

Do not flood a character with detail. Just plan one or two special details that make the character stand out. The details should suggest something about the character. Often the details are the things that we would notice if we met this person. For instance, if she has a thin mouth this suggests that she is cruel! Details could be:

hair – *tousled, ragged, ginger, straggling*
nose – *pointed, sharp, bulbous, red*
mouth – *thin, tight, smiling, pinched*
teeth – *crooked, two missing, jagged, like tombstones*
eyes – *blue, piercing, sharp*
walk – *hobble, dancing step, limp, march*
hands – *gnarled, arthritic, wrinkled, like claws*
clothes – *red jeans, trim suit, brown leather handbag*
spoken expressions – *"that's the ticket", "watcha sunbeam"*
pastimes – *looking after snakes, watching* Star Trek *videos, collecting beer mats*
special skills – *can see into the future, spits a long way; juggler, singer*

Encourage children to make lists in writing journals of useful details, words and phrases. They can keep these as a store to use in future stories.

Characters' feelings

Before the class start writing, ask them to give their main character a feeling. Brainstorm a list of possible feelings, for example:

miserable
angry
happy
jealous
determined
lonely.

The children should decide how their character is feeling and why, e.g. 'She is angry because her Mum shouted at her.' They must remember to keep thinking about how the character is feeling during writing. This helps the writer to decide what the character says, how they say it, and what they might do next, for example:

Sal glared at her Mother.
"I'm going upstairs now," she yelled.

Character types

A different approach to selecting a feeling is to choose character types. It can help to have two characters who are friends – but make them contrasting types, e.g. shy and bossy. This will lead to conflict! Types could include:

the leader
bossy
happy-go-lucky
boffin
sporty
keen
always in trouble
troublemaker
sneak
friend-splitter
loner
bully
big-head
dreamer
over-friendly

Key character questions

To help trigger a dilemma in a story, you could ask the class to think about any of the following when planning – take each in turn and discuss possible ideas.

- Wish – what does she really want?
- Fear – what is he afraid of?
- Lie – she has told a lie.
- Secret – he has a secret.
- Warning – she has been told not to do something.
- Mistake – he has done something wrong.

Any of these options might lead into the plot.
 Summarise what has been learned, e.g. when planning a character think about the following:

- an interesting name;
- one or two details that suggest something about this character;
- how the character feels (and why);
- what 'type' the character is;
- key character questions to help start the story.

Other quick advice is to:

- have one or two main characters, not a gang;
- keep it simple;
- have a goodie and a baddie;
- base characters on people you know, with a bit of invention.

Workshop 2 – characterisation through saying and doing

You do not need too much description

Show the following passage and ask the class to discuss what is wrong with it. Can they work out which sentences are actually needed for the story?

Jez peered into the tunnel. He was a tall boy for his age and had blond hair. He was dressed in a pair of new jeans and a blue tee shirt. He had brown eyes and freckles on his cheeks. He had on a new pair of trainers. His hands were slim and his mouth was a thin line of determination.

"Come on," he called to Slim, "let's go in."

Tease out that the description is over the top. It intrudes into the story and holds things up. The only bit that helps us to know something about the character is, *his mouth was a thin line of determination*. The key part of the story hangs around what is said and done – too much description can get in the way of telling the tale. All you need is:

Jez peered into the tunnel, his mouth set in a thin line of determination.

"Come on," he called to Slim, "let's go in."

Show character through what is said

Show the following sentences for the children to discuss. Ask them: How is the character feeling and what sort of person are they? How do you know?

"Get out," she snarled.
"Where do you get that?" said Sam eagerly.
"Get over here at once," demanded Mrs Rost.
"Sim's got more than me," whined Sal.

Character is revealed through what is said, and how. Ask the children to write down something that a character might say who is:

angry
sad
cruel
happy

Beware! Some children end up writing a string of speech and it can be easy to lose track of who is speaking. Show the children the following and ask them to discuss why it is not well written.

"Hello."
"Hiya."

"Hi."
"Good to see ya Gaz."
"Yea."
"I think I should go to the shop."
"I don't want to."
"OK, you stay on guard."

The writer has given no clues as to who is speaking. And the reader cannot picture what is happening, as we are not given any information. Demonstrate how to 'infill' between speech, showing what the speaker does as they speak, followed by what the listeners do.

"Hello," said Gary, as he sat down on the park bench. Jez and Jules ran up, panting for breath.

"Hiya," shouted Jez.

"Hi," chimed in Jules. She stared at Gary through her new glasses, "Good to see ya Gaz." Everyone laughed.

"Yea," smirked Gary. Jules looked different in her new glasses.

"I think I should go to the shop," mumbled Gary. He took off his old glasses and stared at the broken lens. The others looked at each other.

"I don't want to," said Jules. She'd spent enough time there for one day!

"OK, you stay on guard," said Jez, pointing to their school bags. She grabbed Gary by the arm and began to steer him in the direction of the optician.

Writing tips

- Do not overuse speech adverbs, e.g. he said cruelly, she replied kindly, he said sarcastically, etc.
- Do not overuse speech verbs, e.g. she snapped, he objected.
- Balance the use of said, strong speech verbs, and speech adverbs.

Show character through what is done

Show the following two passages to the children. Ask them: What do they show about the characters? How do you know?

The dog raced towards the children. Shania stooped down and patted it. Picking up a stick, she threw it as far as she could. She laughed as it raced after the stick.

The dog raced towards the children. Tina stood her ground and waited. As the dog approached she raised her hand and hit out. The dog yelped.

Character is revealed through the choices that characters make – what they do and how they do it. Using the same incident, and opening sentence, ask the children to rewrite it, but make the character very shy – shown through what and how they behave. They are not allowed to write *She was shy!*

Summarise what has been learned: Characterisation comes through what characters say, how they say it, what they do, and how they do it. When you are writing keep thinking, 'Now, how would this person react, what would they say?'

Workshop 3 – showing rather than telling

Ask the children to discuss the difference between these two sentences.

Tim walked through the graveyard. He felt dead scary.

Tim raced through the graveyard, his heart thudding. He paused by a tombstone and peered into darkness. He could feel his legs shaking. What was that dark shape ahead of him?

The key difference is that the first sentence just tells the reader – and telling has no power to move the reader. The second sentence shows that the experience was frightening by using concrete description, powerful verbs and sense impression so that the reader is there alongside the main character. The question also draws the reader into the scene. When developing character it is important to show and not tell how the characters feel and think.

Acting out character

Get the children to work in pairs. They act out and develop a brief scene in role. They should decide what feeling or type they are and let this influence what they say and do. For example: a child has stayed out playing too late and comes into the kitchen – Mum/Dad is waiting.

As a class, observe different pairs. Guess what feeling or type is being portrayed – and discuss how this was put across. Then demonstrate how to turn this into a short piece of writing – without resorting to telling, e.g. *Dad was cross.*

"Hi, Mum!" called Toby, sauntering into the sitting room. He flopped down on the sofa. "What's on telly?"

"Where on earth have you been?" snapped his mother, glaring at him. She strode across the room and turned the TV off. She stood in front of him, her arms folded like a sumo wrestler. "Well?"

After your demonstration, ask the children to work in pairs to turn their scene into writing. Those who finish should find good examples to read aloud to the class from their current reading book – especially where the dialogue or action reveals character. End the session by children reading their own writing, or extracts from books. The class have to say what the character is like – and what clues give them away.

Summarise what has been learned. Where possible, emphasise that writing should show how a character feels, through what they say and do.

Writing tips

- Think of a good name.
- Use a few special details.
- Decide how your character feels.
- Show character through what is said and done.

Settings

Workshop 1 – creating settings

Think real

The setting for a story is, of course, an important element. Young writers often leave out any description so that the setting is hard to imagine. This weakens their writing. Many children think that every time they write a story they have to invent something new. However, many writers use settings that they already know. This is a helpful tip, as they can easily picture places that they know – and can therefore use detail to bring the setting alive. Adding in a dash of extra invention may be needed – but the key is to use detail.

Helping the reader build up a picture of the setting – where the story is taking place – has many similar traits to characterisation. A little description is needed because too much might interrupt the flow of the story. The reader will fill in the detail from their own imagination.

Discuss some of these ideas with the class. Does anyone know any stories where the writer has used a place they know well? (For example, *The Wreck of the Zanzibar* by Michael Morpurgo, set in the Isles of Scilly, where he holidays each year.)

Name the setting

To build up a setting, talk the children through the workshop. The first thing that is worth doing is making a collection of names of different places. The right name can help to bring a setting alive for the reader. For instance, *Hangman's Wood* sounds as if it might be dark and rather frightening – just the right place for a ghost story. Swap ideas and begin an ongoing collection in their writing journals.

Be precise

When planning the setting, it is no good being vague. For instance, if you ask a child where their story is going to be set the answer may well be 'America' – this is useless. What is needed is a precise place – exactly where are the characters? Spend some time listing possible settings that might be included in a story. Ask the children to say exactly where the main character is. For example:

> sitting on the bench at the bus stop
> standing in the queue at the chippie
> waiting in the church doorway
> waiting outside the school gates
> on the back seat of the school bus
> on the corner of North Street, by the railings...

Now ask the children to mention one detail that they would notice if they were at the setting. This could be something that can be seen, smelled or touched. For example:

> The green paint on the bench is peeling.
> The smell of vinegar...
> The dark oak door creaks.
> Crisp packets blow in the gutter.
> The seats are made of shiny, slippery leather.
> A spider's web glistening in the sunlight...

Decide the time of day

The place itself is not enough. Now ask the children to decide the time of day as well. After all, if a character is waiting outside the school gates at lunchtime that creates a familiar setting, but if it is midnight then the setting takes on a different tone.

Describe the weather

Move on to thinking about the weather (or season). Create a quick list of possible weather conditions, and use a little description including a powerful verb, personification or a simile. For example:

> Rain lashes the streets.
> Thunder booms.
> Snow drifts.
> Crisp air, fresh as lemon…
> Cold wind bites into my face.
> Sun beats down, and the road shimmers.

Spend some time brainstorming short descriptive phrases for different types of weather. Collect these in the writing journals to be used as an ongoing resource bank.

Bring the setting alive

The key to bringing the setting alive is to use detail and sense impressions. Exactly what can be seen and what can the character hear or smell? Sometimes not much description is needed, as the setting is unimportant. For example:

> The two boys wandered across the school hall and into the classroom.

Nothing else needs to be added. Sometimes a little detail can help to build up a picture, if the setting is unfamiliar to the reader. For instance, use the following extract with the children. Underline in one colour parts that describe the setting. Annotate points that provide clues about the character.

use of familiar setting — is she a dreamer? — familiar description

comfortable setting

e: young nager?

> Sally lay on her bed and stared up at the cracks in the ceiling. The crazy network of spidery cracks in the plaster had amused her for hours as a child. Now she could see nothing in them. From downstairs the sound of the TV mumbled on. Leaning up on to one elbow she reached out and picked up her make-up mirror. She stared at her face, wrinkled her nose, and grinned.

she has grown up

sound to create setting

concerned about her looks

feels content

use of detail to bring character alive

Now write up the following bland description on the board.

> Corky rushed into the storeroom. It was a big room. It was dark. It was dirty. There was a load of stuff in there. He had to hide.

Ask the children what they think of this writing. Is it good? Why not? How can it be improved? Demonstrate how to develop the setting, using details and sense impressions. For example:

> Corky rushed into the storeroom. It was large as a barn. For a moment he paused and peered round. At first he could see very little, but soon his eyes became adjusted to the gloom. He clambered over a large trunk, dust clogging his throat. He wanted to sneeze but he knew that he had to keep quiet. In a corner something rustled. Corky paused but the noise disappeared. So, he struggled over a pile of canvas bags, broken deckchairs and old camping equipment and made his way to the darkest corner. He had to hide soon or they would find him.

Work together on the following scene, developing the setting, and then let the children take their own ideas and write a short scene in which a character rushes into their setting.

> Tim rushes into the shop. He crosses the floor and picks up something to buy.

If the children find it hard to select detail from memory or to invent detail, then use location writing. Take them to any nearby place – even if it is just the roadside – and train them to look, and to locate details. They should jot these down using clipboards. Back in the classroom, the children can create a short scene using the details gathered.

✏ Writing tips

- When writing a setting, use the place but also the time of day and the weather.
- Use details and sense impressions to help bring the setting alive.
- Base settings on well-known places – but also invent.
- Let the settings suggest something about the character.

Workshop 2 – scary settings

Writers use settings to create atmosphere and manipulate how the reader feels. Ask the children to list possible comfortable settings, e.g. the kitchen or their bedroom. Then ask them to list possible scary settings, e.g. a deserted house at midnight!

To write a really good paragraph with a frightening setting, teach the children to introduce an element of tension in one of three ways.

1. The characters hear something suspicious, e.g. footsteps, a twig snapping, a scratching noise.
2. The characters see something odd, e.g. an eye, a hand, a shadow moving.
3. The characters sense that something is not quite right, e.g. they feel they are being watched.

The children will need to employ some of the following strategies.

- Use short sentences to create tension and make the heart beat quickly.
- Balance the short sentences with longer ones containing detail.
- Don't reveal what makes the noise – keep the monster hidden – just reveal a shadow or a glimpse. Keep the reader wondering.
- Pick out unusual detail to describe the setting, creating atmosphere.
- Mention the darkness or cold.
- Have the main character ask a question or think aloud, e.g. *"What was that?" hissed Sim.*
- Describe the character's reactions to show how they feel, e.g. *His hand gripped the banister till his knuckles turned white.*

Make a checklist of the above points. Then use the following paragraph to demonstrate how to create a scary paragraph in which the setting creates tension.

why is she being careful?

someone might hear

why no rush?

why? who or what moved it?

cold = ghosts!

suspense words

alliterat – sound ghostly

shows how character feels

to give emphas

I made my way <u>carefully</u> up the stairs, <u>one step at a time</u>. Even though I wore my soft shoes, the <u>boards creaked</u>. In the <u>silence</u> of the <u>empty</u> house, the sound seemed explosive. At the top of the stairs, I paused. A bedroom <u>door</u> swung open. A dark <u>shadow shifted</u>. <u>Dust shimmered</u>. A draught of <u>cold</u> air touched my face.

"Get a grip," I thought. <u>But</u> the door swung back again, too quickly, and I knew that someone had to be there. <u>I could feel my heart thudding</u> as I <u>gripped</u> the poker tightly. <u>I stepped forwards</u>.

short sentence for impact

Now use shared writing to write a similar paragraph, describing a setting and making it scary. Provide a simple frame for the paragraph. For example:

- The main character enters the setting.
- The main character moves through the setting.
- The main character finds something important and unexpected in the setting.

Read and analyse the following passage and then imitate it in shared writing.

The garage door creaked open. Something scuttled into the darkness but I stepped in and began to pick my way through. A cobweb brushed my face. I stifled a scream. My heart thudded and as I made my way forwards, it grew darker and colder. Old newspapers, brown paper bags tied with string, cardboard boxes, and ancient, moth-eaten rugs that smelt of mothballs littered the floor. It was like stepping through a maze with the lights turned off! Thick dust powdered every surface, tickling the back of my throat. I stopped at a pile of old newspapers. And it was there that I saw the hand. It was quite still – and white. At first I thought that it was marble. A beautiful, white marble carving. But then it moved.

To help trigger what is found, ask the children: What is hidden? What is dangerous? What looks unusual? What is out of place?

Writing tips

- Use the setting to create atmosphere.
- End stories by taking the characters to a safe place like home.
- Make settings frightening by having the characters sense that something is not quite right.
- Pick out unusual detail to describe the setting, creating atmopshere.

Workshop 3 – settings in different types of story

Different types of story rely on different types of setting. To start this workshop, provide a grid and see what sort of settings the children think are typical of the following four types of story:

1. fantasy – e.g. magical garden, wayside inn, dungeons, magical towers, beaver's lodge
2. science fiction – e.g. spaceship, different planet, space station
3. historical – e.g. castles, London streets, lonely moor, the poorhouse
4. traditional – e.g. forests, towers, castles, tunnels, lakes, cottages.

Then show the following basic paragraph which has a bland setting.

Tara walked into the next room. There was a table down the middle of the room. Pictures hung from the walls and a mirror. On the floor was a carpet. In the corner there was a tank of fish. Light came from the windows. The curtains blew in the breeze. Tara stared at the things on the table.

Now work with the children to rewrite the paragraph, as if it were each of the four types of story. To do this, brainstorm possible details, e.g. what might be seen or heard. You might wish to demonstrate for the first type of story. Make a swift list of possible details. For example:

long, silver table
pictures of elves dressed in green-and-red tunics
and dark wizards
mirror edged with leaves of gold
woven pattern of flying dragons
miniature whales
stained-glass windows – splashes of blood-red
and gold
velvet curtains
ivory box of wands

Now show how to rewrite the paragraph using some of the details. For example:

Tara walked into the next room. There was a long, silver table down the middle of the room. Pictures of elves dressed in green and red tunics hung from the walls as well as a mirror, edged with leaves of gold. On the floor lay a carpet woven with flying dragons. In the corner stood a tank of fish – but when Tara looked closer she realised that they were tiny whales, dipping and diving in their own miniature ocean. Light came from the stained-glass windows – sending splashes of blood-red and gold across the room. Dark velvet curtains blew in the breeze. Tara stared at the ivory box of wands on the table.

Use shared writing to work in the same way with two of the three remaining story types. Children can work independently to transform the paragraph using the fourth and final story type. Compare results – what works well? Can you put in too much detail?

Writing tips

- When children are creating settings, they need to think about the genre and what is typical.
- Too much detail can swamp a story – a few details will be sufficient.

Openings

Workshop 1 – writing opening lines

Write these sentences on the board and ask: which opening sentence is more effective and why?

> Sim was walking to school.
> "Just jump," roared Sam.

Take feedback. The second sentence is more effective as it makes you wonder what is going to happen.

In groups, children sift through a pile of books to find:

- opening sentences that are dull;
- opening sentences that make you want to read on.

Each group reports back to the class on the best opener and explains why, taking into account what effect the writer is creating.

Take some of these favourites and categorise them. Some common categories might be:

- **time**

  One winter's evening, when the snow fell thick as feathers, a child wandered out of nowhere into a village.

- **name**

  Billy Craddock was having none of it.

- **exclamation**

  "Gravella, stop that!" screeched Mrs Jarmin.

- **question**

  "Is that room tidy?" Mrs Burdfoot yelled up the stairs.

- **dialogue**

  "Let's go down to the dump," said Tom.

- **warning**

  "Listen here you two – you are not allowed to go to the dump!"

- **wish**

  "Why couldn't I have a Gameboy, everyone else in our class did."

- **scene-setter**

  On the edge of the town stood a factory where no one ever went.

- **traditional**

  Once, not twice, but once upon a time lived three sons.

- **the new arrival**

  Her name was Fiona and everyone thought that she was a snob.

- **dramatic action**

  The bomb exploded at exactly half past twelve.

- **introducing the monster**

  Most people think that ghosts do not exist.

Take each opening sentence type and invent several more based on the same sort of sentence pattern. For example:

> One winter's evening, when the snow fell thick as feathers, a child wandered out of nowhere into a village.

> One summer's day, when the sun beat down, Melanie set off for town.

Ask the children to invent some of their own under the different categories. These should be written into their writing journals so that they may be used when story-writing.

Summarise what has been learned, e.g. a good opening will:

- catch the reader's interest;
- make the reader want to read on.

Workshop 2 – writing opening paragraphs

Opening paragraphs can be used to:

- weave in background information;
- intrigue and tease the reader;
- suggest that something is going to happen;
- introduce the main character;
- introduce the main problem;
- create atmosphere.

The opening should leave the reader wondering what will happen and raise questions in the reader's mind, e.g. why is she feeling like this? It can help to drop in 'hooks' to tantalise the reader. For example:

Claire tiptoed past her brother's door. She especially did not want to wake him.

There are three main types of opening paragraph: character, setting or action.

- Ask the children to work in groups to read opening paragraphs from a selection of books and to choose the most effective. They should be ready to read their favourite and explain why it is effective.
- End the session by listing what you have learned about writing opening paragraphs.

Workshop 3 – character openings

Before writing, ask the children to think about the main character's name, how they are feeling and why. Also, where is the main character and why? Encourage the children to use writing to show how the character feels. Demonstrate with an opening paragraph such as the following:

powerful verbs show he feels angry

short and long sentences for effect

...teration

Sam <u>stormed</u> across the playground. He <u>glared</u> through the railings at the <u>cars cruising</u> down Tuffley Way. His hands <u>gripped</u> the <u>black bars</u>, turning <u>white</u> at the knuckles. He stood <u>like a prisoner staring</u> out.

...ows feels ...nse

image to show he is trapped behind bars – of his anger?

contrast of colour

why is he cross?

Follow the demonstration by shared writing and then independent writing. Other options:

- The children might want to make the character seem unusual by using detail.
- They could 'hide the character' by using a pronoun (e.g. he or she) and leave the reader wondering.

Workshop 4 – setting openings

The description of the setting should be used to create an atmosphere. This can be done through using the senses – especially what is seen or heard – and mentioning a few specific details. It helps to make the setting fascinating in some way. The opening paragraph could end by introducing the character or making something dramatic happen. Demonstrate with a paragraph such as the following:

who is here, where are they?

powerful verb to create pictures

short sentences for dramatic impact

where are we?

empty word to build suspense

sounds unpleas<u>ant</u>

powerful verb to bring senses alives

A <u>fly crawled</u> up the <u>dusty</u> windowpane. <u>Something scuttled</u> into a dark corner. A <u>broken</u> chair lay beside the pile of <u>old</u> carpets. The air smelled <u>musty</u>. From the back of the room, where it was quite <u>dark, came</u> the sound of <u>scratching, scratching</u>.

sense of decay

darkness = fear!

complex sentence to add extra information

repetition to build suspense – what is scratching?

Follow the demonstration by shared writing and then independent writing. The children could try brainstorming possible objects, sounds, or smells in a given place and using these in their writing. Other options:

- The children might use some detail from settings that they know well – but also invent some parts.
- They should ensure that they use proper names for places. Encourage them to let the name suggest something about the place, e.g. Darkwater Hall.

Workshop 5 – action openings

The action could be very dramatic, or just enough to get the story going. The characters could be placed in a difficult situation or in trouble. To lead into this, make a list of things that might go wrong at school or home. Use this list as a basis for writing. Then, demonstrate with a paragraph such as the following:

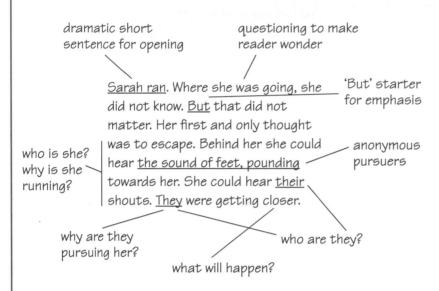

dramatic short sentence for opening

questioning to make reader wonder

'But' starter for emphasis

Sarah ran. Where she was going, she did not know. But that did not matter. Her first and only thought was to escape. Behind her she could hear the sound of feet, pounding towards her. She could hear their shouts. They were getting closer.

who is she? why is she running?

anonymous pursuers

why are they pursuing her?

what will happen?

who are they?

Follow the demonstration by shared writing and then independent writing. Other options:

- The children might introduce the main character doing something reasonably ordinary, but drop in one clue that suggests that:
  - something important has just happened (*they stared at the column of smoke*) or
  - might be about to happen (*that bridge is never going to take the weight of anything too large*).

✍ Writing tips

- Use the opening to catch the reader's interest.
- You could:
  - introduce the main character
  - create an atmospheric setting
  - start with an exciting action.

Paragraphing

Objectives:

Y3 T1 Text 2, 15: begin to organise stories into paragraphs; use paragraphing to present dialogue in stories.

Y3 T2 Text 1: investigate story openings and endings, and use in own writing.

Y3 T3 Text 2, 11, 13: refer to significant aspects of the text, e.g. opening and build-up; write openings linked to or arising from reading; use paragraphs to organise the narrative.

Y4 T1 Text 15: use paragraphs in story-writing to organise and sequence the narrative.

Y4 T2 Text 3: understand how paragraphs or chapters are used to collect, order, and build up ideas.

Y4 T3 Text 12: write an alternative ending for a known story.

Y5 T1 Text 1, 15: analyse the features of a good opening; compare a number of openings; write new scenes or characters into a story in the manner of the writer, maintaining consistency of character and style, and using paragraphs to organise and develop detail.

Y6 T2 Text 1, 2, 10: understand aspects of narrative structure, e.g. how paragraphs in a short story are linked together or how authors handle time; analyse how individual paragraphs are structured in writing; use different genres as models to write short extracts, sequels, additional episodes, or alternative endings.

Y6 T3 Text 7: annotate passages in detail.

Workshop 1 – resolutions and endings

It is most likely that children coming up into Year 3 will have a basic understanding of how to end stories – tying up the tale, sorting out the main dilemma, solving the mystery – though this may be simplistic.

Once children enter Year 3, it is worth distinguishing between writing the resolution and the ending. By this I mean:

- **resolution** – resolving the story or tying up the tale;
- **ending** – some sort of reflective section that follows the resolution, in which there is a reflection on what has happened in the story.

Adopting this extra distinction helps to add depth to the way in which stories are wound up.

Story endings are notoriously difficult. In terms of children's development as writers, the ending is the last piece to fall into place. Many children resort to endings where it was all a dream or they all went home and had tea! Indeed, many of us can remember that struggle to tie up the ending so that you end up having to cop out! This relates in some way to planning, so that the ending has already been thought about.

Writing resolutions and endings

The resolution ties up the story. Write up the following basic plots. Ask the children to work in pairs, deciding how they would resolve the dilemmas. To provide a model, the first is done for you:

1. Two children get lost at the seaside – the class teacher finds them and they end up getting told off for wandering away from the school party!
2. A dog is cruelly treated.
3. A girl falls into a river.
4. An old lady is tormented by bullies.
5. An old man is granted three wishes.
6. A child gets trapped in a cave.

Take the first plot idea and resolution. Use the following paragraphs to demonstrate how the resolution and ending might be written. Do make the point that the resolution might take several paragraphs to write, but in this instance you are just using one paragraph for the resolution and one for the ending.

hold back what she is looking for as long as possible

shows she did not know where to go

Mrs Wagner had <u>wandered</u> all afternoon up and down the beach. She stood on the beach, her <u>attention</u> caught by the sound of an ice-cream van. A group of children had begun to form a queue. She <u>stared,</u> for two of them looked familiar.

why does this catch her attention?

suggests she is looking for something

simile and alliteration
to show how cross she is

shows
Mrs Wagner's
reactions!

A few minutes later, Tom and Sim were being <u>dragged</u> back down the promenade towards the waiting coach. Mrs Wagner was in <u>full flow, furious as a fire</u>. The boys glanced at each other. Part of them was relieved that at long last they had been found. They knew that wandering off had been daft! But the other part of them was not enjoying the full of force of their teacher's anger. <u>And</u> worst of all – <u>they hadn't even had time to eat the ice-creams!</u>

reflective thoughts about what has happened

gentle comment to contrast with teacher's fury!

typical start to an end sentence

Work on another resolution and ending in shared writing. Then, ask the children to select one of the other resolutions and turn their idea into two paragraphs.

Workshop 2 – endings

Once you have distinguished between resolutions and endings, then move on to further work on endings. A good way to start is by piling storybooks on to children's desks and letting them read just the last paragraph. Do they notice any typical features? What often happens at the end of a story?

Ask some children to read aloud selected endings. You may need to direct everyone's attention to the typical features of an ending.

- Often the main characters head for home.
- Sometimes there is a connection with the beginning – it is worth asking the children to read the opening and final paragraphs.
- Usually there is some sort of comment about the story or the characters.

Collect any useful and typical sentences that might be helpful. For example:

They had already turned for home.
After all, who would ever know what Sam had done?
It looks like we're going to have lots of fun this holiday.

But the sky was bright, and she somehow felt that she was going, at last, in the right direction.
"Come on," said Marcella, "I'll show you the way home."
And when she had finished, she placed the hat back on her head and began to walk back to the town.
Maybe James knew?
She thought back to where it had all begun, and longed to see her friend again.
Skiri and Brocha laughed, "I knew we'd make it!"
Andy said happily, "This place seems different now." And they both thought to themselves, and so are we...

✎ Writing tips

At the end of the story, try to do the following.

- Describe, or show, the character's feelings.
- Reflect on events and perhaps provide a moral.

  – The main character thinks aloud:

  Joanna thought that she had been alone for long enough...

  – The main characters discuss what has happened:

  "You were brave," said Tom.
  "Nonsense," replied Joanna.

  – The narrator comments:

  They had had a terrible day...

  – An adult comments:

  "That was daft!" snapped Mr Jimbala.

- Look to the future.
- Mention some object or detail from the story.

Before writing the ending it is useful to reread the beginning to see if some sort of link can be made. For example:

- Revisit where the story began.
- Comment on what has happened.
- Show, or comment on, how the character has changed.

Showing character change

A useful exercise is to get the children to read aloud the first and last paragraphs as a regular part of the writing process. Commenting on how characters have changed is especially powerful if this is shown through how the characters behave, as well as what they say. For instance, the angry character at the start of a story could be shown to be happy by the end.

Demonstrate with an opening.

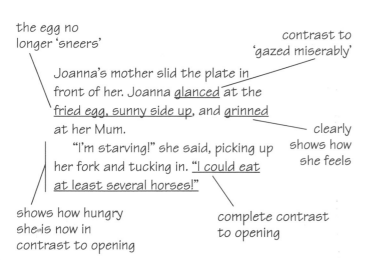

shows how she feels

Joanna <u>gazed miserably</u> at her breakfast. The fried egg seemed to be staring back up at her. And it had a <u>sneer</u> on its sunny face. She <u>stabbed</u> it with her fork, <u>spilling eggy blood on to the white plate.</u>

suggests and reflects her misery and anger

suggests possible future violence

Then demonstrate with an ending.

the egg no longer 'sneers'

contrast to 'gazed miserably'

Joanna's mother slid the plate in front of her. Joanna <u>glanced</u> at the <u>fried egg, sunny side up,</u> and <u>grinned</u> at her Mum.

"I'm starving!" she said, picking up her fork and tucking in. "<u>I could eat at least several horses!</u>"

clearly shows how she feels

shows how hungry she is now in contrast to opening

complete contrast to opening

Ask the children to write the end paragraph to the following opening. They must concentrate on showing that the character has changed through what is said and done.

It was the middle of the night. Everyone lay asleep. Everyone, that is, except for Freddie Pilcher. He lay awake, staring up at the ceiling trying to count sheep. But he never got further than six before the tears welled up in his eyes again. He just couldn't believe it. It was impossible…

Summarise what has been learned.

Workshop 3 – action

Most children – and especially many boys – want to be able to write exciting stories with plenty of action. But it is easy to fall into the trap of cartoon-style writing where the action does not excite the reader. Ask the children whether this paragraph is a well-written piece of action writing.

He ran but they got him. They punched him. He fought with them. They handcuffed him.

Well, it is rather dull. It describes the events but does not make them happen or bring them alive. To bring action alive the writer needs to use powerful verbs and to let the reader see and hear what is happening. Demonstrate to the children how to rewrite the paragraph.

short sentences to create punchy, dramatic impact

'But' opening to create emphasis

cliché suggests violent intent

<u>Sid ran.</u> <u>But</u> within seconds he felt a hand <u>grab</u> his shoulder in a <u>vice-like grip.</u> He spun round. <u>Without warning a sickening</u> punch <u>smashed</u> into his <u>stomach.</u> He fought for breath, doubled up in pain. Somebody <u>seized</u> his hands and the next thing he knew, they had handcuffed him.

dramatic sentence opening

powerful verb

alliterative – violent use of words

impression of physical violence

Now look at writing about being chased, another example of action writing. Again begin by showing a rather dull piece.

He heard them coming. He ran. He got away.

Now take this and demonstrate how to use powerful verbs and the senses to bring the action alive.

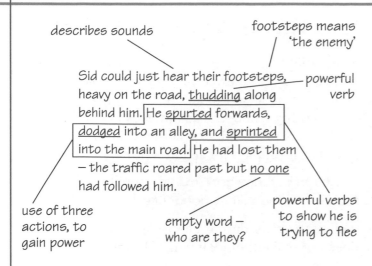

describes sounds

footsteps means 'the enemy'

Sid could just hear their footsteps, heavy on the road, <u>thudding</u> along behind him. He <u>spurted</u> forwards, <u>dodged</u> into an alley, and <u>sprinted</u> into the main road. He had lost them – the traffic roared past but <u>no one</u> had followed him.

powerful verb

use of three actions, to gain power

empty word – who are they?

powerful verbs to show he is trying to flee

Draw up a checklist of points that help with action writing. For example:

1. Use short sentences.
2. Describe a few actions using powerful verbs such as – *grip, grab, seize, squeeze, rush, leap, jump*, etc.
3. Use a sound, e.g. he *grunted, yelled, howled*, etc.
4. Use a sentence with three events to make an impact.

To lead into the children's own writing, set a simple task in which you provide the basic scenario. For example, the main character is being chased – she, or he, jumps on to a bicycle and races down a hill, with the scene ending when the character reaches the bottom of the hill and leaps off the bicycle.

It can even help to give the opening and final lines. For example:

They were only just behind him. Danny grabbed the bicycle and leaped on…

…

He threw the bike to one side and jumped over the wall. He had won himself a head start.

Before the children write, brainstorm the sorts of words that might be useful when writing about riding a bike downhill, e.g. *pedal, quickly, wind, breeze, rush, gasp, eyeballs, sting, squeeze, frown, squeak, metal, rusty, ache, pound, race, zoom, zip,* etc.

Workshop 4 – build-up

The build-up in a story occurs in the space leading up to the complication or main dilemma. It is a short space in which the characters are going about some ordinary event or task, not knowing that things might go wrong. It may be necessary for the writer to move their characters to wherever the action will take place, e.g. if they are going to fall in a canal, the build-up will have to concentrate on getting them down to the canal. Or if, as here, they are going to fly kites, the build-up will need to focus on taking them to a suitable, open space.

The two children made their way down Silverhill, past the fish market and on to the Barn Fields. There they stopped and Sandy tried to fly her kite. It was no good though. Not even the slightest breeze disturbed the leaves.

It can help if the children think about the build-up as one or more bridging paragraphs, which lead into the complication or dilemma. The build-up need not be long but has to position the characters. It can also be used to give further information about the characters, so as to establish the sort of people they are. For example:

Sandy grinned at her friend. "Here, you have a go," she said, handing over the kite. But Laksmi had never flown a kite and rather than make a fool of herself, she shook her head.

Use the following scenarios as a focus for the children to write simple bridging passages. The ideas in brackets offer the further challenge of adding in some specific characterisation.

- Two children cross a field (one is angry).
- One child takes a bus ride (and feels lonely).
- Three children walk to the shopping precinct (one is being teased).
- Two children take a dog for a walk (one is miserable).
- Two boys/girls stack up chairs in the hall (both are being silly).

Workshop 5 – suspense

The suspense paragraph may, of course, be the point at which the story is about to introduce the dilemma – something awful is about to happen. Some stories may have suspense at a number of points, or build it up over time. There are a number of specific devices that writers introduce and use to build up suspense. Let the children read and annotate the following passage – what tactics is the writer using to help build up suspense?

Carys gazed at the bus timetable. Thirty minutes to go! She looked up and down the road and then sat down. She took out her mobile phone and punched in Tim's number. It began to ring and as she cradled the phone between her shoulder and ear, she grinned to herself imagining what he would be doing. Half past six – he would be on the computer right now. She just knew it!

It was then that she heard it. A scratch, a scrape, like claws. It came from behind the shelter. Carys shifted uneasily. What on earth could that be? She stood up and looked back through the grimy window. Something slipped back, quick as a shot, into the darkness. The bushes rustled. Carys knew that someone or something was hiding from her. She shivered, clutched the phone and turned to run. But her way was barred!

Take feedback from the class. Draw up a checklist of useful strategies that they have noticed. Your checklist will look something like this:

- Lull the reader into a false sense of security.
- Then introduce an element of unease.
- Suggest something horrible is about to happen.
- Use 'empty' words (e.g. *it, something, someone*) to hide the monster.
- Delay revealing the monster.
- Use a shadow or glimpse of part of monster.
- Use ominous sounds, e.g. scratching, rustling, thudding, etc.
- Use a question to make the reader wonder.
- Use a simile to build a frightening picture.

- Show the character's reactions through what is said or done.
- Use a *But* sentence for impact.

Now use the checklist as a basis for demonstrating how to write a suspense paragraph. As you demonstrate, keep referring back to the checklist (e.g. 'I'm going to use a question now to make the reader wonder what is whispering'). Occasionally reread relevant parts of the original model and show how you are using the same sort of features.

Slowly, Sasha turned round and stared. She froze, the money bag clutched tightly, as she strained to listen. Yes, a vague tapping from the chimney. And was that a voice whispering? She peered into the gloom and could just see the outline of the cold, stone fireplace. Something darted back in, quick as a blade, up the chimney. Sasha gripped the money bag tighter, without even knowing what she was doing. Perhaps she should run? But it was too late. A cold, dark voice spoke to her…

Let the children comment on your demonstration – how effective is your paragraph? Could it be improved? Then use the checklist for a shared composition, writing a similar paragraph. You will need to invent a character and place her in a lonely place. For instance, you could have a character called 'Karin' alone in a cinema, when all the lights go out.

After this is accomplished, move on to independent writing – draw the children's attention to using the checklist and models for support as they write. Provide different scenarios. For example:

- The main character is alone in school.
- The main character is in a park after dark.
- The main character is lost in a forest.
- The main character is walking home from a club after dark.

Workshop 6 – dilemmas

This is that moment in the story when things start to go wrong. What are the characters going to do? It can happen straight away at the start of the story, if the writer wants to draw the reader into the drama immediately. Many writers leave the dilemma for a short while so that the story builds up towards it, and the reader has had the advantage of getting to know the characters involved – and therefore of feeling some sympathy for their plight.

Let the children work in pairs or threes to list the sorts of dilemmas that are found in different types of story. For example, what goes wrong in:

- traditional stories? – e.g. losing three granted wishes or meeting a fearsome giant;
- school stories? – e.g. getting bullied or losing homework;
- home stories? – e.g. having a horrid older sister or Mum not letting you go camping;
- ghost stories? – e.g. the school hall is haunted;
- mystery stories? – e.g. a child is kidnapped;
- animal stories? – e.g. a pet is taken ill;
- magic stories? – e.g. a child travels to another world and cannot get back.

When taking feedback, check to see if there are any common dilemmas that might cross over between different types. For example:

- getting lost;
- something gets stolen;
- everything is all right and then someone or something horrible arrives;
- defeating the monster;
- overcoming a fear;
- a dream comes true;
- getting trapped or kidnapped.

At this point, it is helpful if the children can look through a few books that they have read and find any dilemma passages – where things start to go wrong. They should make a collection of useful paragraph openers for dilemmas and keep this list handy in their writing journals, adding to it as new ideas crop up. Such openers might include:

> At that moment,…
> Just then,…
> Without warning,…
> With a scream,…
> Nobody saw…
> Silently,…
> Suddenly,…

Then, practise writing paragraphs where the writer injects a new and worrying element. You might demonstrate with the following paragraph.

atmospheric setting

suggests she is in charge

Out of the swirling mist strode Skarla, the huntress. She stood before the crowd and they sank to their knees as if in prayer. But the low moan that let slip from their lips was no prayer. It was the sound of defeat. Nissa knew that they would soon be handcuffed and taken away. She would not be seeing her friends again, unless she could escape.

builds up idea of defeat

explains bleak future

hint of what needs to be done

Follow the demonstration with shared writing and then independent writing. Provide different scenarios. For example:

- trapped in an abandoned car;
- kidnapped in error;
- falling into a river;
- caught by a bully.

Workshop 7 – cliffhangers

The cliffhanger can be a useful tactic, especially in a longer story that is written in chapters. TV series use them all the time, so that each episode ends at a frightening point – possibly with the main character literally hanging off the edge of a cliff – so that the readers will tune in the next week to see what is going to happen. Cliffhangers maintain suspense and keep the reader reading. The idea is to have a surprise event that leaves the character in a terrible position, one that remains unresolved at the end of the cliffhanger section, so that the reader has to read on to the next chapter or section of the story to find out whether they will escape!

Can the children think of any examples of cliffhangers? For example:

- a hand grabs the main character;
- the main character suddenly falls into space;
- a car screeches towards the main character;
- the main character slips at the cliff's edge;
- a gun goes off;
- a car's brakes fail.

Remind the children that the idea is to shock the reader. It can help if everything seems to be OK and then some sudden and unexpected event occurs that places the main character in a perilous position. This can be most effective at the end of a chapter. Demonstrate using a paragraph that starts with everything appearing to be OK, but ends with a last line providing a punch – introducing a situation that leaves the main character in a dreadful position.

sense of relief – she is safe at last

Nissa paused at the top of the diving ladder to regain her breath. It had been quite an effort to climb that far. She stood up on the board and walked carefully out above the pool. She looked down and could see a thousand faces staring up at her. She grinned to herself, for this was her element, her world. Here she knew no fear. In a moment she would dive out, through the air, down into the blue below. She tested the spring of the board and walked back to position herself. At that moment the board sagged down, creaked, and cracked!

shows Nissa is still worried

all is well

problem left to last line

alliteration to catch attention

onomatopoeia to sound like its meaning

Use an idea from the list of possible cliffhangers to compose a similar paragraph in shared writing and then move on to independent writing.

Workshop 8 – flashbacks

Flashbacks are quite a sophisticated technique and you might wish just to explore these with the more mature writers in Years 5 and 6.

In a flashback, the characters are taken back in the story so that the reader can see some previous event that might be significant and be helped to understand what is happening. It can be very useful to use a flashback if the story launches straight into the action. The writer can then take the reader back to some previous event that throws light on what has happened.

It is useful to build up a bank of flashback connectives in the children's writing journals, as these can help to trigger a flashback paragraph.

Remind the children that the flashback has to have a point – it needs to illuminate the current events in a helpful way, or, at the least, show how the characters have changed – otherwise don't bother! Paragraph openers might include:

It had only been two hours ago that…
Jane thought back to the moment when…
A week ago, it seemed like a lifetime. Jane had been…

Ask the class to look at the above examples and start a list in their writing journals. They should then skim through books to find more.

Set a scenario and demonstrate a flashback. For instance, pretend that the main character has got lost in a forest because she ran ahead from the main group.

That morning they had been told not to run ahead. Mrs Forest had been quite clear.

'You can get yourself lost in Sharpham Woods without even trying,' was what she had said. Nissa had shaken her head, sensibly agreeing, eyeing the boys who were winking at each other and muttering about exploring. The big adventurers! And here she was, a few hours later, completely lost, having run ahead like a baby! She was furious with herself.

In shared writing compose a similar paragraph and then move on to independent writing. Provide a different scenario. For example:

- The main character has lost a gerbil.
- The main character has dropped some money.
- The characters have stayed up late to watch TV.
- The characters are lost in a town.
- The characters are stranded on a beach.
- The characters meet a giant.

Workshop 9 – paragraph changes

Show the following paragraphs and ask the children to discuss why the writer begins new paragraphs.

On the other side of the forest the giant had lain down to sleep. He placed his knapsack to his side and began to doze. Soon, the forest was filled with his rumbling snore.

An hour later he woke with a start. Something had woken him up. He looked round, peering into the trees. Giants do not have good eyesight and Farshore was no exception. He could see nothing in the dark shadows beneath the great redwood trees.

Shawlin, the goblin, sighed. He watched the giant struggle to his feet and begin to search around for the knapsack. It hadn't been too hard to steal it. And as long as he kept under the protection of the shadows, the giant would never see him.

A scream split the air. Farshore had stepped on to a dog's tail and the poor hound set up a terrible hullabaloo. It threw back its head and howled. Farshore stooped down and stroked the dog, muttering kind words which actually sounded more like a rusty organ-grinder than a giant. How ashamed he felt.

Take feedback. The first paragraph establishes the place. But the second paragraph signifies a change of time, the third paragraph a change of character, and the fourth a change of event.

Then, underline the different paragraph openers that could be used in other situations. Write up the headings below.

> Change of place
> Change of time
> Change of person
> Change of event
> Change of speaker
> Other reasons…

Use a pile of books on each table and ask the children to add to the collection of paragraph openers, under the different headings. Can they find at least five useful openers for each column? They should especially look out for connectives that writers often use.

A good list of paragraph connectives can be very helpful for those who struggle with story-writing. Paragraphs in narrative are small scenes. It can greatly help young writers to see each paragraph as a mini-scene.

A few headings can suggest how to structure a basic story. For instance, using 'Humpty Dumpty' as a model can provide a simple story framework of four scenes, each heralded by a few words to tune the writer into the structure. For example:

1. All day long Humpty sat…
2. Suddenly, he…
3. There was a terrible crash…
4. Everyone tried…but…

Now compose the four paragraphs in shared writing.

A simple tale of quest might be given a basic frame of a few scenes by using connectives to structure the tale. For example:

1. Introduce character:

   Once upon a time…

2. Set task, e.g. go to shops:

   One day…

3. Character sets off:

   As she walked…

4. Character arrives:

   Once she reached…

5. Character decides what to do next:

   So she decided…

When the children are reading, ask them to identify why a paragraph changes. They should keep adding useful connectives to the lists in their writing journals and use these when planning, structuring and writing their stories. It is also worth having a large wall list of common narrative connectives and calling upon this list to help write.

✎ Writing tips

- Use paragraphs to describe each scene.
- Reread each paragraph to help you write the next.
- Look back at your plan to check what happens next.

Style

Objectives:

All sentence-level objectives relate to children developing their writing style – using words effectively, controlling and varying sentences for effect, ensuring stories cohere and using stylistic devices such as simile. Certain text level objectives highlight style as well.

Y3 T1 Text 1, 2: select words and phrases that describe scenes; how dialogue is presented in stories, e.g. through statements, questions, exclamations.

Y3 T1 Text1: collect phrases and sentences for story openings and endings.

Y3 T2 Text 1: investigate the style of traditional story language and collect examples for use in own writing.

Y3 T3 Text 2, 11: refer to significant aspects of the text, such as the opening, build-up, and atmosphere, and know that language is used to create these, e.g. use of adjectives for description; focus on language to create effects, such as suspense, mood, and scene-setting.

Y4 T2 Text 5, 10, 13: understand the use of figurative language, e.g. similes; make use of work on this and on adjectives to describe settings; write own examples of descriptive language based on those read, and link to work on adjectives and similes.

Y5 T1 Text 15: write new scenes in the manner of the writer, maintaining consistency of style.

Y5 T3 Text 3: write in the style of the author.

Y6 T1 Text 6: manipulate narrative perspective by writing in the voice and style of a text.

Y6 T2 Text 2: analyse the success of texts and writers in evoking particular responses.

Y6 T3 Text 1: describe and evaluate the style of an individual writer.

Workshop 1 – using words

Write these sentences on the board and ask: which of these sentences is the most effective and why?

> The cat sat on the mat.
> The Siamese cat curled up on the Persian rug.

Take feedback. Most will say the second sentence because the words bring the picture alive. The verb is more powerful and the nouns more precise. Make the point that writers choose their words with great care. Words are like magic spells – they bring pictures into the reader's mind. These can be powerful pictures or faint images. It all depends. The rest of this workshop takes a quick romp through different types of words and makes a few points about using them to write effectively.

Nouns

Which creates the stronger picture – *dog* or *Rottweiler*? When using nouns, the writer may select something precise that names the object. For instance, there is a world of difference between:

> He picked up the book.
> Tim picked up his copy of *Harry Potter*.

As a class, quickly brainstorm possible precise alternatives for the following bland nouns:

> dog – *poodle, dachshund*, etc.
> cat – *Siamese, moggy*, etc.
> car – *Skoda, Mercedes*, etc.
> flower – *sunflower, bluebell*, etc.

In story-writing, names of characters and places are very important. Keep an ongoing class list of interesting names for characters and places. You need names that conjure up an image. For instance, the name *John Hunt* does little for me, but a name like *India Opal Buloni* sounds exotic, exciting and different – it comes from Kate DiCamillo's book *Because of Winn-Dixie*.

Adjectives

Adjectives are another useful part of any story-writer's equipment. You will want to encourage less mature writers to use adjectives. The next step is for them to choose interesting adjectives – and to avoid repetition. Once they are tuned into selecting unusual and interesting adjectives, you may find that they begin to overuse adjectives, so that their writing sounds overwritten. This final stage involves selecting adjectives that add something new to the noun which the reader needs to know.

To open the debate about adjectives you might use a series of sentences to tease out the main points. Write these sentences on the board and underline the nouns in one colour and the adjectives in another. Ask the children to comment on the writer's choice. Build up a checklist of points about using adjectives – see brackets.

> The small, black-and-white, fierce, excited, yapping, rough-haired dog barked.

(Don't use too many adjectives.)

The tired, weary, sleepy cat dozed.

(Don't use adjectives that mean the same thing.)

I posted the thin envelope into the red letterbox.

(Don't use adjectives that tell the reader what is obvious.)

The big policeman grabbed the big burglar by his big arm.

(Avoid repetition.)

She turned the key in the rusty lock.

(A well-chosen adjective tells the reader something new – and important.)

Ask children to begin a collection of interesting adjectives in their writing journals. These could be written in once a week and gathered from reading.

Verbs

Most story-writers would say that their main writing tools are nouns and verbs. Verbs give the action to writing – they bring scenes alive. They let us know how people think and feel. Write the following sentence on the board.

Trent went to the shops.

Discuss which is the weak word – most children will identify the verb as being especially feeble!
Now change the verb. For example:

Trent staggered to the shops.
Trent skipped to the shops.

Discuss how this affects what we might think about the character. In the first sentence, *staggered* suggests that Trent may be weary, sick or in pain. Whereas, in the second sentence, *skipped* suggests that Trent may have just won the lottery!
During reading, alert the children to the use of powerful verbs. When marking their writing, underline weak verbs in order to indicate that they must think again and select something more effective. In their writing journals, they should begin lists of verbs to use, for instance verbs instead of *said, went, look, ate*, etc.

Adverbs

Adverbs perform the same sort of function for verbs as adjectives do for nouns. (Adjectives might be better known as 'adnouns'!). Adverbs add to the verb, helping to refine the meaning. Use these sentences to help identify some writing points about using adverbs. Underline the verb in one

colour and the adverb in another. Then discuss and draw up a checklist of points – see brackets.

The robber raced carefully, cautiously, calmly, bravely down the road.

(Don't use too many adverbs.)

The rat raced quickly, hurriedly, speedily home.

(Don't use adverbs that mean the same thing).

The girl whispered quietly.

(You don't always need an adverb, if the verb is well chosen – the reader already knows the girl is talking quietly).

Danny tap-danced clumsily.

(A well-chosen adverb adds something new that the reader needs to know.)

The message with adverbs (as with adjectives) is simple – choose carefully! Encourage the children to collect adverbs in their writing journals under these headings:

How adverbs – slowly, quietly, cleverly, happily, etc.
Where adverbs – here, there, away, outside, etc.
When adverbs – now, yesterday, soon, later, etc.

Choosing words to make interesting sentences

To end the workshop, take several sentences and see what can be done to them by:

● adding in extra words
● changing words to intensify their meaning.

For instance, how could these sentences be improved, or made more vivid or dramatic?

The snake went across the table.
He walked past the shop.
The girl ate the sandwich.
"Let us leave here," she said.

The sentences might be reworked, respectively, as follows.

The angry adder slithered across the kitchen table hissing.
Arnold marched pompously past the empty skateboard shop.
Tania Carotta chewed thoughtfully on her smoked salmon sandwich.
"Run for it!" yelled Skater frantically.

Workshop 2 – varying sentences

Make sure that you pile several storybooks of reasonable quality in front of each child. Now write the following passage on the board and ask the children what they notice. Is it well written? Is it good writing? What is wrong? Why doesn't it work?

Tom ran down the lane. He strode into the shop. He ordered a bag of sweets. He paid the shopkeeper. He walked outside. He saw the bus. He ran for it. He caught it.

The main problem is that all the sentences sound the same – they are the same sort of length and constructed in the same way. They all start in the same way. This can become very boring for the reader who needs variety. This workshop introduces the idea of varying sentences for different effects. Every now and then, the children can scan through the books on their tables and search for examples. Explain that the writer can vary sentences by many different means.

Using questions

See who can find a place where a question is used. Obviously questions are asked in dialogue – but what about in the rest of the text? Questions are useful because they make the reader start wondering and draw the reader into the characters' way of thinking. For example:

What was that slipping between the shelves? Tom leaned forwards…
Why did Kerry keep asking questions?

Using exclamations

Exclamations are useful for being dramatic. Can anyone find examples? List a few. When are exclamations used? Often, as in these two examples, at the exciting or dramatic part of a story.

They were doomed!
"Help!"

Using short and long sentences

The passage that we read at the start of the workshop has too many short sentences. It needs some longer ones to balance the rhythm and add in extra description. Short, simple sentences are useful for clarity and being dramatic. If you want your writing to be exciting or to contain suspense, you will need to use some short sentences. For example:

She stared.
They crept forwards.
They spun round.
It was dead.

Getting the right balance between long and short sentences can be hard. Constant rereading helps, so that the writer can hear when the shorter sentences need a longer one. As a rule of thumb, two short sentences will probably need something longer, as here:

Tom ran down the lane. He strode into the shop. He went up to the counter, spent some time staring at the jars of sweets, and then ordered a bag of humbugs.

Using varied sentence openings

The opening passage sounded like machine-gun fire partly because all the sentences start in the same way. Provide a checklist of openings for the children to use. As you write each one on the board, the children should imitate them and create their own examples. Make sure to draw children's attention to the use of the comma.

To vary openings:

- use an adverb

  Slowly, she turned round.

- use a verb with -ing (non-finite verb)

  Rushing down the stairs, she tripped.

- use a verb with -ed (non-finite verb)

  Amazed, Tom turned round.

- use a prepositional phrase

  Down the lane, came the ambulance.

- use a simile

  Like a grin, the moon shone.

- start with a connective

  Although they were tired, the children pressed on.

- reorder the sentence

  Across the river the swan flew gracefully, like snow in the breeze.

Ask the children to see how many different ways the final sentence can be written!

Using compound sentences

Compound sentences are joined by and, or, but, and so. They contain clauses of equal weight. For example:

I like tea and I like coffee.

This sort of sentence is useful in writing because it is easy to read (the word *and* makes few demands on the reader!) and it helps writing to flow and move forwards. Can the children find any examples in the books? Of course, many children get stuck at this stage, using an endless stream of sentences joined by *and then*. They can be helped to avoid this if they build up a bank of different connectives, and learn how to find other ways to connect sentences.

Using complex sentences

If the children are going to write anything that has depth, then they will need to use some complex sentences. These are sentences that have a main clause and one or more subordinate clauses. The subordinate clause cannot stand on its own and relies on the main clause. It is an extra piece of information that has been tacked on to the main proposition. It is handy to have a checklist of common subordinating connectives for the children to use as a word bank, e.g. *after, although, as, as if, as long as, as though, because, before, if, in case, once, since, though, till, until, unless, when, whenever, whereas, wherever, while.*

Ask the children to take some of these words and find sentences using them in books. They should then try to imitate them. For example:

Although the bonfire still smouldered, Simra left it burning.
Although the Mercedes was parked carefully, Tim was worried that it might be stolen.

End this workshop by rewriting the original passage, using some of the different means of varying the sentences, in order to make it more engaging.

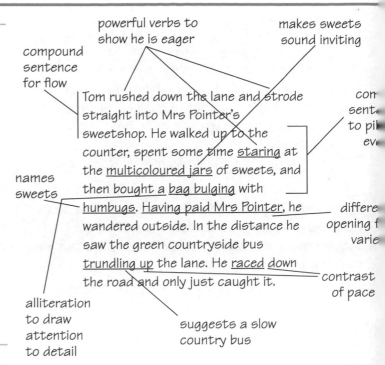

powerful verbs to show he is eager

makes sweets sound inviting

compound sentence for flow

names sweets

alliteration to draw attention to detail

Tom rushed down the lane and strode straight into Mrs Pointer's sweetshop. He walked up to the counter, spent some time staring at the multicoloured jars of sweets, and then bought a bag bulging with humbugs. Having paid Mrs Pointer, he wandered outside. In the distance he saw the green countryside bus trundling up the lane. He raced down the road and only just caught it.

suggests a slow country bus

contrast of pace

different opening f varie

Workshop 3 – using stylistic devices

Young writers can call upon their paintbox and add a dash of colour to their writing by using a number of different devices.

Playing with sound

The easiest effect that they can call upon is alliteration. This is where words that are near each other start with the same sound. Alliteration draws the reader's attention to whatever is being said: it is used to make sentences (or parts of sentences) memorable, which is why advertisers use it, e.g. *Buy British Beef*. Take some sentences and add in a few words to alliterate. For example:

He wandered outside.
He wandered wearily outside.

Then ask: can anyone find an example of alliteration in their reading book?

The other important device for playing with the sound of a sentence is onomatopoeia. This is where words are used that sound like their meaning. For example:

The gutter gargles.
The bees buzzed busily.

If children are writing well, they will use onomatopoeia anyway – especially if they choose their words carefully. It is helpful to collect words or phrases that sound like their meaning, so that the children have a storehouse to call upon as they write.

Creating pictures in the reader's mind

On of the most powerful ways in which a writer creates a picture for the reader is by using similes. Explain that a simile makes a comparison, saying that one thing is like or as another. The children will have met similes in poetry and should begin to use them sparingly in their own story-writing.

As a class, start collecting effective similes from reading and make quick-fire lists of new similes to call upon. For example:

> A cloud is like … a dark stain.
> The moon is like … a silver fingernail.
> The sun is like … a giant's angry eye.

Also spend time listing similes that use *as*. For example:

> As thin as … a rat's whisker.
> As quick as … a slip on a banana skin.
> As bold as … a barrel of monkeys.

The second way to make a picture is by using metaphor. Metaphor is more powerful than simile. It says that one thing *is* another.

Simile (uses *like*): The moon is like a smile.
Metaphor (does not use *like*): The moon is a smile.

Note that a metaphor does not use *like* or *as*. For instance, a shy person or heavy snow might be described in these ways:

> She twitched nervously, was a mouse in the office.
> The snow was a blanket across the city.

Of course, we often use metaphors when we are talking. For example:

> 'You rat!'
> 'She's an elephant.'

I once overheard a Mum say to her son, 'You big donut!'

There are many expressions that use metaphor, such as:

> the mouth of a river
> tongues of flame
> education is a political football

One form of metaphor is to use personification. This is when the writer pretends that an object, animal, or idea has human qualities and uses a verb that would normally be associated with a human. For example:

> The wind moaned.
> The moon smiled.

Make a long list of verbs that are associated with human actions, e.g. *smiled, grinned, laughed, chattered, whispered, danced, skipped, sneezed*, etc. Now list objects around the room and use the verbs to create a simple list of sentences using personification. For example:

> The tables grinned.
> A chair sneezed.
> The carpet complained bitterly.

Can anyone find any similes, metaphors or personification in their books? Ask children to start collecting examples from reading poems and stories. In the classroom set up a board for 'image' of the week and encourage children to invent their own images. Practise this by choosing a simple subject, such as the fog, snow, rain, wind or sun, and seeing who can create a simile, metaphor, and personification. Here are three respective examples:

> The fog drifted down the lane like a snake.
> The fog dragged its grey body across the moors.
> The fog sneaked into houses and stole through doors.

Listed below are the ideas of children in the Year 6 class at Mount Nod Primary School, Coventry.

> As still as the queen's guards!
> The water punched and kicked the rocks as they stood by helplessly!
> The shadow's owner was a ghostly, grey galleon of cloud and moon!
> I sank down into the dark abyss of the cellar with saliva dripping from the monster's jaws.
> When I came to, I saw two angry eyes staring at me which actually turned out to be two huge hospital lights!
> Outside it was war; the lightning winked; the thunder roared; the wind whistled wildly whilst the hotel stood stump-still!
> With eyes like pins with balls of fire in them!
> The snow's white coat filled every crack and cranny as the wind whistled a mournful tune.
> Whilst staring down at the everlasting floor as it scrolled past him.
> The wind howled like a wolf in pain and the crisp air pinched and prodded at anyone who walked the mist's maze.

Workshop 4 – changing viewpoint

Place a pile of books on each table. Ask the children to sort the books into two piles: stories written in the third person (using *he* or *she*) and those in the first person (using *I*). They will discover that most stories are written in the third person. A few stories are written in the first person – probably the best-known author who writes in this way is Jacqueline Wilson. Listen to an example of each – perhaps a paragraph or two read aloud.

● What is the difference?
● How does writing in the first person make the reader see things? (It can help the reader to identify with the main character powerfully.)

Advise the children that usually a third-person story is easier to write. However, if they decide to write a first-person story they must keep rereading to check that they have stayed in the same person and not slipped back into the third person.

A useful way into this area is to set up a small piece of 'hot-seating'. You need to use two characters – the main character and a narrator. Set up a scenario, e.g. the main character has pushed someone over in the playground. The two children have to tell what happened from their viewpoints. In this case, the main character speaks in the first person and the narrator in the third person.

Main character I was cross with Tim. He kept shoving me in the game so I pushed him over.

Narrator Tim had been shoving Josh all through break. In the end Josh lost his temper and he pushed Tim over.

Now introduce the notion that, when writing, it is possible to show events from different viewpoints. Ask the children: How did the teacher view the events? What about Josh's sister or Tim's best friend? If children use this notion in their writing, it can help if they change paragraph when they shift the viewpoint.

Use the following storyline to practise writing from different viewpoints. Two children are playing with a ball. The ball goes into the road. One child runs after it. A car is coming down the road...

Split the class up so that they write from different possible viewpoints. Faster writers should attempt two viewpoints.

The child who runs into the road Sandy kicked the ball right at me. I think that she was in a mood with me. Anyway, it rolled on to the road. I was in such a hurry that I didn't think to look up the road...

The child who does not I was furious with Jaz for scoring so many goals. He always has to win. So I booted it as hard as I could. He just spun round and...

The driver I wasn't thinking about anything much. The radio was blaring and I was whistling along. I noticed these two kids kicking a ball about, so I slowed down. Then the ball shot into the road and I knew what was going to happen, so I...

A bystander Sandy and Jaz were playing football at the end of Hardy Avenue. The ball rolled out into the road. Jaz...

The mother, looking out of a window I just looked up at that moment and saw Jaz step out into the road. He never stops to think before he acts...

When the children write, ask them to drop some clues into their writing that suggest something about the character. From the examples given we learn that Jaz likes to win and doesn't always think before he acts.

Of course, in a story the writer would only use one or two viewpoints. Demonstrate how to take this scene and provide two different viewpoints so that it sounds like part of a story:

shows how she feels

shows Sandi's view of Jaz

- Choose your words carefully.
- Use precise nouns and powerful verbs.
- Use adjectives and adverbs with care.
- Vary sentences to create different effects.
- Use stylistic devices to make your writing vivid.

Sandy <u>scowled</u> at Jaz. She <u>grabbed</u> the ball, placed it on the ground, and took several paces back. <u>She'd had enough of Jaz scoring so many goals and then strutting around like a peacock</u>. She rushed at the ball and with all her might <u>slammed</u> it at Jaz. It shot past him, straight on to the road.

reinforces her anger at Jaz

paragraph shift

 At that moment, Mrs Carver happened to glance out of the kitchen window. The scene seemed to freeze. Her two children and the ball skidding on to the road. And then, as if in slow motion, Jaz rushing, as reckless as ever, headfirst into the road.

Carver's erent view he event — on Jaz

cliché to show scene and suggests an accident is about to happen

delaying telling the reader what will happen

gives a view about Jaz being reckless

End the session by looking at the way the narrator can comment, adding a different viewpoint. This can be a helpful way to add in extra layers of information or help the reader understand the characters. For instance, using the above example, the writer might conclude the scene by using the narrator to comment by 'stepping outside' of the story.

shows reader the whole view of the car and the mother and the children — like a camera's longshot

powerful verb echoing the screech of a voice

As the car screeched to a halt, Mrs Carver's mouth formed a silent scream. The two children would never know that moment of terror. What they would know was her anger, when five minutes later they were standing in the kitchen, getting the telling-off of a lifetime! None of them noticed the driver sitting at the side of the road sobbing...

quick shift to safety

camera moves back to the driver, ignored by the others

Different types of story

Objectives:

Y3 T1, 2, and 3: stories with familiar settings; myths, legends, fables, and traditional tales plus stories with related themes; adventure and mystery stories.

Y4 T1, 2, and 3: historical stories; stories about imagined worlds, sci-fi, fantasy adventures; stories that raise issues, e.g. bullying, bereavement, injustice; longer stories.

Y5 T1, 2, and 3: short stories; myths, legends, fables, and traditional tales; stories from a variety of cultures and traditions.

Y6 T1, 2, and 3: classic stories; stories from different genres; extended stories.

Workshop – playing with story types

There are many different types of story:

> traditional tales
> myths
> fables
> legends
> anecdotes
> diaries
> thrillers
> chillers
> adventures
> mysteries
> animal tales
> magical tales
> school tales
> domestic tales
> science fiction
> fantasy

They all have their own typical features. When planning to work on a type of story it is worth teasing out the typical features explicitly – what sort of settings, characters, events and dilemmas arise in this type of writing? Each type of story will have its own typical vocabulary, grammar and tone. To draw children's attention to this idea you could play a guessing game by supplying them with some sentences from different story types. Ask them to name the type of story and explain how they know. For example, what clues are there in the following sentences?

> Long ago there lived a King who had three sons.

> Carrie stared into the darkness but all that she could see was the cold, misty outline of a shape drifting down the hall.

> Carter spun round, his hand gripping the revolver.

> Jenny crouched down by the pony and stroked its head.

> The Zarg's ship appeared on the screen and then disappeared into hyperspace.

> Mrs Himes did not like mice but her son, Barry, did.

> A bright light crackled from his wand, while the unicorn's horn glowed.

> Charmaine wondered why there was a light on in the empty house at midnight.

Once the children are familiar with a few different types of writing, they may find it amusing to write a short story that moves between story types. Read the following short story through. What type of story does each paragraph represent? What clues give the type away? Extract the basic storyline and then use demonstration, shared and independent writing – or ask the children to write in groups to create different versions, shifting between narrative types.

Once, not twice, but once upon a time, there was a young Prince called Hal who was summoned by his father, the King. The King commanded him to take a magic lamp to his sister, who lived many miles away.

Hal caught the first train that he could. As he boarded the train he noticed two men, dressed in long coats, getting on. One of them had a jagged scar on his cheek. It was the Maltese Falcon, the most feared gangland criminal in the dockside area. And Hal knew what he must be after.

That night Hal locked himself into his train compartment. The train thundered on through the night towards its destination. Suddenly the lights in the compartment flickered and plunged Hal into darkness. He stared out of the window at the flickering town lights, as the train rattled onwards. It was cold sitting in the compartment, alone. Something in the corner rustled. Hal thought that he could hear breathing. But he was alone. It was then that a hand touched his face. A cold hand. Cold as death!

Hal screamed and, grabbing the compartment door, burst out into the corridor. A young child was standing outside, holding a puppy. Hal's training as a vet would stand him in good stead. "Come here, little fella," he muttered. His gentle hands felt the puppy's leg. "You need a splint old son," he said. The boy grinned in gratitude.

At that moment the two men appeared coming down the corridor. Hal left the boy and his puppy and ran to the guard's carriage. He was alone in there. Alone, that is, except for the latest ST4 Trident Warzipper. He clambered into the pod and pressed the evaporator. The craft shimmered, disappeared, and then reappeared hovering above the train. With one touch of the moduliser he was in hyper-travel.

Sooner rather than later Hal reached his journey's destination. Hal gave the lamp to his sister who was very happy. The moral of this tale is that the fastest travel always beats the snail.

The sections, or paragraphs, from the tale above run as follows.

1. Traditional opening – the main character is given a task.
2. Detective narrative – the main character sets off and is chased.
3. Ghost narrative – the main character meets a ghost.
4. Animal narrative – the main character finds a wounded animal.
5. Science-fiction narrative – the main character hitches a lift in a spaceship.
6. Fable ending – the main character arrives and a moral is made.

Writing tip

- Adapt your writing style and contents to the type of story.

Quick-fire story ideas

The ideas listed below are tried and tested ideas for story writing. When using ideas to trigger a story, it is important to dress up the stimulus wherever possible. This may mean using first-hand experiences, posters, visits, pictures, music, objects, creatures – anything to stimulate the imagination. It is the difference between saying, 'you find a ring' and passing round a collection of coloured rings. These ideas will need further dressing, but can act as a useful source to trigger story writing.

1. There is a noise in the night – what is it?
2. The teacher draws a monster on the board – suddenly it comes alive and slithers off the board!
3. There is a rumpus around the back of the school – a dragon has landed.
4. The main character wakes up and has changed into someone else, e.g. a teacher or parent.
5. A child wakes up with a superpower.
6. Write down an animal, a person and an object. Write a story which includes all three.
7. The main character finds a ring and slips it on – it is magic!
8. A dream begins to come true.
9. A teacher has a secret and a child finds out.
10. A child enters another world through an opening, e.g. a door, window, trapdoor or mirror.
11. A child is trapped in an old house.
12. A wish comes true.
13. The main character tells a lie.
14. Two children find a wishing machine.
15. Two children shrink and fall through the floorboards.
16. A child finds an invisible cloak.
17. The main character finds out that they can make magic.
18. A parcel or letter arrives containing something mysterious.
19. Write a story to explain an expression, e.g. 'A Frog in my Throat', 'Ants in my Pants', etc.
20. How the leopard got its spots.
21. Supposing you could...fly!
22. What if...a tree could talk!
23. A father boasts that his child can turn wool into gold.
24. The main character meets a talking owl.
25. You find an alien stranded and frightened.
26. You get stuck in a nightmare.
27. Your computer starts talking to you.
28. An inventor creates a potion that turns people into zombies.
29. A toy comes alive and is evil.
30. A teacher tries to make the class do her will.
31. You go to a sleepover and someone breaks into the house.
32. A local ghost story starts to come true.
33. You get trapped in a haunted house.
34. You become trapped inside a computer game that has become real.
35. You discover that you have a twin – an evil twin –and you get the blame.
36. Someone takes your photo and there is another figure in the photo.

37. You get transformed into a creature.
38. You go camping and your friends disappear, one by one.
39. The main character is bullied.
40. The main characters are doing something they enjoy. But a dog appears, barking madly, and runs towards the main characters. They have to react swiftly.
41. The main characters disagree and an argument begins. Each want their own way. They might split up. They begin the story feeling in a bad mood.
42. An adult is telling the children off. They have done something wrong and are in trouble. Perhaps it was not really their fault. Maybe they have to put things right.
43. The main characters find something special. It is so special that they are not sure what to do with it – or how to keep it safe. Others may want to get it.
44. The main characters find that they have lost something special. They have to find it swiftly. They dare not ask anyone else.
45. One of the main characters reveals that they have stolen something. What should they do? Can they put it back? Should the friend sneak?
46. Two children get lost in a wood or town. They find, or overhear, something that leads them into danger.
47. A local bank is robbed and the main character finds the house where the robbers are hiding.
48. A new schoolgirl is kidnapped (who is she?) and the main characters find a clue that leads them to where she is held prisoner.
49. The main characters get trapped in an old house where a gang of spies is planning to kill the Prime Minister.
50. A friendly inventor creates a way of turning mud into gold. The formula is stolen. The main character breaks into the robber's house and steals it back.
51. Write a story that is built around two of these characters.
    a) This character is happy-go-lucky. They don't mind much what they do, don't get into a huff easily, and enjoy life. They are fun to have around.
    b) This character is shy. They are quiet, don't like to push themselves forwards, and often feel nervous with other people. They may have strong views. They are often lonely.
    c) This character is feeble. They often get pushed around by others, quickly give in,

and follow the crowd. They could easily be led into trouble.
    d) This character is very positive about everything. They always look on the bright side of life, make others feel good, and crack jokes.
    e) This character is aggressive. They make sharp comments, have a quick temper, and push others about. At times, they may be a bully.
    f) This character is a natural leader. They like to make the decisions, organise other people, and think they are right. They lead the way in all situations.
52. Write a story that begins in one of these settings.
    a) This story begins in school – perhaps in the classroom or playground. It is after lunch. The children are playing. It is near the end of the Christmas term, and cold outside.
    b) This story begins at home – perhaps in the kitchen. It is early morning and everyone is getting ready for school. Outside, the rain pours down.
    c) This story begins in the town centre – perhaps in the shopping arcade, on a bustling street or at the park. It is an early summer's evening.
    d) This story begins in a forest. Trees tower high and a path winds ahead. There is a clearing with a deep pool. It is getting dark and stars are coming out.
    e) This story is set in the countryside – perhaps by a stream or on a hillside. It is a dark night and there is snow falling. Distant lights flicker from the village.
    f) This story begins at the seaside. It is a hot sunny day in the holidays. There are people everywhere. The sea is quite calm. An ice-cream van is nearby.